Stop Wasting Time

The Manufacturing Practitioner Series

Stop Wasting Time: Computer-Aided Planning and Control

Norman Sanders

Stop Wasting Time

Computer-Aided Planning and Control

Norman Sanders
Illustrations by Einar Engebretsen

Prentice Hall
New York London Toronto Sydney Tokyo Singapore

First published 1991 by
Prentice Hall International Ltd
66 Wood Lane End, Hemel Hempstead
Hertfordshire HP2 4GR
A division of
Simon & Schuster International Group

Typeset in 11pt Palatino by IDOC Publishing Services, Norway.

Printed and bound in Great Britain.

Library of Congress Cataloging-in-Publication Data

Sanders, Norman.
    Stop wasting time: computer-aided planning and control/Norman
Sanders.
        p.   cm.
    ISBN 0-13-850462-8
    1. Industrial project management—Data processing. I. Title.
HD69.P75S325 1991
658.4'04'0285—dc20   91-27063
                                                                                    CIP

British Library Cataloguing-in-Publication Data

Sanders, Norman
    Stop wasting time: Computer-aided planning
    and control
    I. Title
    658.400285

    ISBN 0-13-850462-8

---

1 2 3 4 5   95 94 93 92 91

To Luca Di Montezomolo

Head of the Organising Committee,

Italia 90, World Cup

Who said:

Italy has made crisis a fundamental instrument to pass from
planning to implementation of projects.

9th June 1990

Take courage Signor Montezomolo, it isn't only Italy, it's
everywhere.

Contents

Contents

List of Figures

Preface

A word from the last of the pioneers

There aren't many of us left who were privileged to be around with nothing to do when the first computers started to work, and, by definition, if you were around at the start you had no choice but be a pioneer, even if you didn't care for arrows in your back. I was one of the privileged few, and though my back may be bristling I have enjoyed these forty years beyond all expectation. A pioneer by nature, my constant fear has been that the pioneering would soon stop. All the problems would be solved and I would have to take up the training of performing elephants. But that hasn't happened. Looking back on it all we have done the easy things, tough though they seemed at the time.

At first, in the 1950s, reliability; keeping the computer going and getting it to print the right numbers. Then, by 1960, speed; a thousand mind-boggling printed lines a minute. But what were the engineers doing with all those numbers? By great good fortune I found myself working for the world's biggest computing pioneer, Boeing, when the profits from the 707 started rolling in. These seeded the 727, which became the first ever to be built by later what became to be known as computer-aided design. Though we didn't actually call it anything, we just did it. Heady stuff. An enormous and very obvious return on investment.

At the same time the airlines were evolving their booking systems, the computer thereby establishing itself as the basis of the modern industrial world; the twin pillars of manufacturing and information handling.

The 1970s seem now to have been a decade of consolidation; a steady calm after the big bang. Most of the obvious economics were taken care of, and big computing matured into a profession at one level and a well-understood service at another. While costs fell steadily year by year.

The less obvious economics, but perhaps the greater, were the possible use of computers by managers. That's where the future of computing lay, and there seem to be three interweaving strands of development leading to it; coping with creative people, handling working-level detail in a structured way and making computing cheap. The solution to the first problem eluded us for a decade or more. The problem was the unpredictability of managers, hence the difficulty of writing computer programs for providing them with their answers. We didn't know the questions. The bottom level of any organisation is highly predictable, rhythmic, structured and most amenable to specification. But as you move up the corporate layers time-spans increase, structure gets hazier, and personal opinion replaces collective practice. At the working level the computer program stays with the function. But at the managerial levels programs, such as they are, move with their owners from function to function.

Pioneering in the 1970s consisted of inventing data structures and linguistic tools that enabled programs to be written on the fly as the need arose. From months to seconds. That's where the pay dirt lay. Eventually we were successful. By the middle of the decade the concept of a relational database came about, and by the end of the decade we had profitably working examples. The 1980s were poised for the Holy Grail of computing - the computer terminal sitting on the desk of the company president. All we had to do was fight our way into the head shed.

The second, parallel, and at first quite independent process, was the evolution of project management technology. This started on paper in the 1950s with the Polaris submarine project, and computers were brought into play by about 1960. The pay dirt here was the enormous value of large projects, and the consequent costs of delay. If you could manage a project properly you could save millions.

The going was slow though, and it wasn't until about 1977 that a really usable system became available. And it coincided with the Moe Report, an epochal investigation into the reasons why apparently similar projects in the North Sea petroleum industry took such widely different times to carry out, resulting in such widely differing costs. As a result, project management offshore since 1980 has been intimately tied to the computer.

The project management system that set the standard for the industry is called Artemis, and it had the historic good fortune to employ a relational database at its core right from the start.

The petroleum industry paid for the development of Artemis and similar systems. Here was the primary payoff, and it was done mainly on relatively large equipment. But the third strand in the story emerged in the early 1980s, the power and cheapness of the personal computer. By making cheap versions of project management systems the technology was transferable to the rest of industry. By about 1988 these cheap versions had become very powerful, and the stage was set.

I don't think anyone would claim to have brought about the combination of the general management strand and the project management strand deliberately, or even to discern their eventual combination. But it happened. The key to the problem is the fact that most of the value of a company lies in its projects, hence top-level concern for their health. The key to the solution lies in the relational database. And the key to the cheapness of the solution lies in the personal computer.

This book is therefore an apotheosis of computing and management. It is based entirely on experience and prejudice. I spend my entire working day trying to establish systems, and I write these lines in airports. I don't, however, hold out much hope of immediate impact. I think that a project manager who understands his subject might find some useful hints if he isn't already way ahead of me, but my experience of general managers leaves me only modestly hopeful. I have been messing about with computers since 1950, and lecturing and writing about them since 1960, but it isn't easy. The reason is that you simply have to experience these things to understand them and benefit from them, but the people you are preaching to are where they are primarily because of their proven ability to delegate to others. So perhaps the best ploy here is to issue a plea for sympathy. Try it please, just for my sake. Put a stop to all this pioneering and let me retire in peace. Do it properly, and then let me know if you have managed to tear yourself away from it.

There is light at the end of the tunnel, however. There are definite signs now that the technology is following the path of biological evolution and is creeping onshore from the deep. The technology is being transferred from the wet to the dry, from the large to the small and from the modern to the traditional. In my own case I have had the extreme good fortune recently to develop systems for the milk industry, specifically Elopak Ltd., an international company that builds dairies and manufactures cartons as an alternative to bottles. The project technology is identical to that of the offshore industry, but the application is very different; large numbers of small projects spread around the world as opposed to single large projects assembled in one place. The professional opportunity of working with managers in a way that would have been unthinkable a decade ago because of computer costs.

My hope is that by the turn of the millennium the PERT (Project Evaluation Revue Technique) chart planning network will be central to everything a company does; that all computer systems will be related to it, and that all levels of management will understand it and use it as naturally as breathing. However, I think there is one item of technology still lacking which will sabotage this hope if we don't get it fairly soon. So let me finish with a crie de coeur.

Today's typical PC contains 120 megabytes of data, and we can expect this to be increased by the time this ink is dry. But there is space for only 2,000 on the face of the standard screen - less than 0.02% of the capacity of the computer. This allows for at most half a dozen planned activities to be displayed; only a small fraction of a network. This makes network manipulation a very tedious process. It's like examining an elephant with a microscope. What I've been asking for for years is a flat screen to hang on the wall, some six of today's screens wide by four deep, say. This would allow us to display a complete network of a hundred activities. Attached to it I would like to have a sort of super mouse allowing us to move the activities and constraints about by direct contact rather than at the keyboard. I want to conduct my discussions on my feet, not at the keyboard with my back to the project team.

We don't want to display all 120 megabytes, but even one half of one percent would be an enormous improvement. Please keep this in mind as you read these pages, and take every opportunity of needling the industry, who traditionally attack the wrong problem. They have started to solve this one, but there is a long way to go yet.

In summary, then, this book is about projects, about management and about computers. It is addressed to project managers, the general managers of the companies they work for, as well as the computer operators who do the work at the keyboard. Sometimes the material is aimed at one more than the others, but I hope it is of interest to all three nevertheless. I hope it's readable, and if so I hope it helps you to be a bit more profitable.

Acknowledgements

> When we mean to build,
> We first survey the plot, then draw the model;
> And when we see the figure of the house,
> Then we must rate the cost of the erection;
> Which if we find outweighs ability,
> What do we then but draw anew the model
> In fewer offices, or at last desist
> To build at all?
>
> *Shakespeare, Henry IV, Part1*

In thanking those who helped me write this book I would like to start at the beginning. The beginning was the computer, without which so much modern technology would have remained but theory. And the beginning of the computer was Charles Babbage, one of the great minds of the nineteenth century. I would like to thank him for inventing the ideas that led to the realisation of the computer in the twentieth century, and to Maurice Wilkes who made a computer that actually worked. From that point on theory quickly led to practice, enabling me and thousands like me to enjoy a life of crunching numbers. We have all influenced one another, but there isn't space here to mention everyone. I especially thank those who have made an impact on the subject of this book, the business of making plans and trying to carry them out.

This book would not have been possible without the software that it describes. Today there are many software tools available, and all of them seem to work well. They are the latest result of years of evolution, and many people were involved, but it was James Miller, the inventor of Artemis (the language, not the goddess) who made the breakthrough. James laid the framework of an industry, providing a career for thousands. Roy Brown, the specifier, tried to restrain James from reinventing the world, while Richard Evans, the catalyst, with them saw the need and carried the result into the world of business. As with all success stories, the few quickly become the many, and I no longer know them all, but I am grateful for what they have done.

Given the hardware and the software the rest of the story is about applying the technology to the working world. Perhaps that's the hardest part. To be successful requires a knowledge of both computers and people, how they work and how to make them work in greater harmony. Here I find myself surrounded by some very special people. They are both philosophers and action men and women. A rare combination. Those who helped me write the book, both directly and indirectly, were Tony Piper, valued colleague of many years, Arthur Berg Reinertsen the visionary who doggedly sticks to his visions, Patsy Williams who knows everything including the fact that cakes are all the same size, Jarle Oygarden, Grant W. Erwin Jr. and Ian Pyle who manfully waded through the entire thing and made profound suggestions for its substantial improvement, and Stephen Taylor who very kindly made the plots. The production of this book was, in itself, a project, and we used the computer throughout. As a result it was finished ahead of schedule. I would like to end by thanking Knut Skog for making it possible to go from keyboard to camera ready copy automatically by means of his excellent book composition system.

For purposes of fluency in this book I give the appearance of having made the unacceptable assumption that all managers are male, and that all secretaries and data entry people are female. However, nothing is further from the truth. There are, today, of course, lots of lady managers, and throughout, the use of his means his or her.

In the old days we used to thank forgiving secretaries for suffering through the manuscript. But one of the unforeseen results of computers has been the (to my mind indefensible) decision that we don't need secretaries now that we have word-processors. So I lost Tamzin Howell half way through, leaving the rest of the book to be typed by the world's slowest typist. I think the whole thing is a gigantic conspiracy to stop people writing books.

Chapter 1

The Mess in Your Kitchen

A General Anarchy Prevails in my Kitchen

Samuel Johnson, September, 1778

If you haven't actually had your kitchen refurbished, or, worse, tried to refurbish it yourself, you certainly know other people who have endured the ordeal. Or if not a kitchen, a bathroom or an extension to your house. Or you may even have lived through the horror of having an entire house built for you.

Do you remember it? That gaping hole where the old sink used to be. Weeks trying to wash up in a small plastic bowl. "Sorry Guv, we ran out of sink units. Had to order a special supply from Poland." The Danish taps, delivered before the job started, and hopelessly lost by the time the pipes were installed. And that was late because the plumber was busy. Plumbers are always busy - but never with your work. Have you noticed that? But I hasten to assure you that it isn't with my work either. Indeed, have you ever met the person the plumber is doing the work for?

And the electrical work? You waited weeks for both of them, the plumber and the electrician, and then the Great Day arrived when they both turned up simultaneously on your doorstep and spent the next few weeks in each other's way, except when drinking tea, made by you on the primus, and exchanging reminiscences of triumphs of yore, of cullinary disasters stretching back to apprentice days, punctuated by the occasional granny flat or basement sauna.

And the brick work? "Sorry you can't park your car, Guv, but it's agin regulations to dump the bricks in the road." The driveway is blocked for months because they delivered three times as many bricks as they needed, and left you to dispose of them - after billing you for the whole load.

The driveway is blocked for months

And the carpentry? Sawdust all over the house. A vast surplus of nails accompanied by a shortage of the teak panelling. "Comes from South Africa actually Guv. They call it Swedish so that people will buy it, but it comes from South Africa. Supplies are somewhat spasmodic, and the different batches never quite match."

"April?", the painter roars with laughter. "April? Did Fred tell you April?" His laughter dissolves into violent and painful coughing. He sits down and mops the tears of mirth streaming from his beady old eyes. "What with these jokers I won't be able to start before June. And then I'm taking the missus and kids to the Costa Brava the whole of July. I told Fred that before we started the job. If you could help me by taking your holidays in September, I reckon I could have this little jobby finished by October. April?! Cor, old Fred's a right one he is."

And the carpenter dissolves into another paroxysm of laughter that echoes to Heaven where there must surely be a special place for builders; a vast unfinished paradise stretching to eternity, accompanied by a symphony of sound of saws, hammers, blow-pipes and the merry slapping of paint. The ninety-nine percent club engaged upon their last assignment.

But if there are any builders reading these words, I didn't mean builders I meant welders. My secretary can't read my writing.

And you thought it only happened to you? Or you thought it only happened on the domestic scale? Or you thought it only happened in Britain? Have you ever lived in Italy? Do you know what it's like to have a heap of pulverised marble on the kitchen floor accompanied by a rusty gurgle from the tap and no light to see by to fix anything? Have you never had to shave in wine? Or America, where the walls are so thin they won't support the shelves if you actually put anything on them? Or France, where you can't complete a phone call pleading for help? Or Yugoslavia where they drink slivovitz all day and leave you without a single ninety-degree corner in your entire house? Or Russia where they have yet to invent the plumb-line?

To approach this whole discussion from another angle, can you imagine the calm and exquisite sense of control that permeates the headquarters of any major corporation? Perhaps you've even experienced it. All is relaxed. All is charm. All is well ordered. All is clean and shiny. The key is everywhere low. The talk is of the price of the stock that day. And if it has gone up it is only because the market is totally unaware of the chaotic reality at the working level - as is the management itself in many cases.

Management is the management of plumbers, and to the extent that managers don't manage, plumbers don't presumably know what to plumb, nor painters paint nor carpenters carp. Actually, the plumbers I have met are much better plumbers than their bosses are managers. The carpenters I have watched wring miracles of cutting and fitting. The plasterers create surfaces that only Euclid dreamed of. And how the electricians thread all those wires through all those wall cavities, connect them up, plunge the offices in light and fill the factory floor with the whirr of machinery, I really cannot fathom. The whole thing is a miracle of pragmatic interaction that the artisan, I suspect, takes great pride in, and management, I know, the credit for.

But rarely is management justified in taking this credit. Rarely are the implementers of a project given a plan to work to, and their management, thereby, a yardstick to be judged by. Most work carried out on the surface of this planet is unplanned.

Heresy, I hear you cry. We invest millions in planning. We have a moving five-year strategic plan to steer the corporation into a rosy future. We have a two-year building plan to ensure adequate factories and offices. We have a six-month computer plan which we review in microscopic detail every month. We have a corporate director of planning, and departmental planning groups; and everyone's success is judged by comparing achievement against a plan. We plan every breath we take. No surprises at our place.

You call it planning. But is it really? Does a net flow of money constitute a plan? Or is it the result of a plan? And what does the plan look like that the money stream is based on? Aspirations or concrete activities? And if the latter, how well are they described? And how accurately are they related? How complete are they? Where are they displayed? On the factory benches? On the board room wall? How often do you refer to them? Are they hallowed scripture or are they action documents? Are they something to hoodwink the banks with, or are they reliable information to the working level to help them do the job properly?

How often do you report against them? And how often do you change them in the light of sober experience?

Today, in industry and commerce the answers to these questions are lamentably inadequate. Not everywhere, but in most places. The shining exception is the oil industry, and in particular the offshore industry. But generally speaking, the quality of planning is appallingly poor, and the basic principles almost universally unknown. The purpose of these chapters is to rectify this situation, and to suggest some simple methods of obtaining a much better handle on your corporate activities, even to the extent of using a computer. The computer techniques have been with us for twenty years, and in the last ten we have seen a steady development of their use in very large organisations. The techniques are now well honed, and the price of computers has dropped to the point where they are universally available.

The renovation of your kitchen, from chaos to completion, is an example of what we call a project. And the rest of this book will be about how to use modern techniques for planning and managing projects successfully; in particular how to use computers to make these techniques even more powerful. No prior knowledge is required of computers, and we promise not to frighten or mystify you with jargon. All will be revealed in seductive simplicity.

The important point to make in this chapter is that a project starts and finishes (you hope) and consists of a sequence of activities - rip, smash, mix, slosh, bend, weld, hammer, paint, pay - carried out by appropriate people - rippers, smashers, plumbers, carpenters, painters and you - (sometimes several at the same time), - all in an orderly progression, requiring such resources as bricks, plaster, pipes, planks, paint and cheque book.

Activities, resources, time and money, all tied together in a little adventure.

All in all it's very simple, as the following pages will show. So if you continue reading you will discover how to obtain a return on investment that surpasses anything you've ever dreamed of.

Chapter 2

Projects Ancient and Modern: An Information Explosion

I Only Ask for Information

Dickens, David Copperfield

The mess in the kitchen is something we can see and perhaps understand, even if it doesn't elicit our entire sympathy. And albeit the individual agony imposed upon the family is unbearable, if it were confined to the domestic front it wouldn't warrant the attention of expensive technology nor the writing nor reading of this book. But it isn't. Industry is in a far worse mess than your kitchen, and what has always puzzled me is that people buy shares in it.

Your kitchen is a miracle of order and tranquillity compared to the problems of building an offshore platform, for example. They both get finished in the end, but because you aren't close to the detail of the latter, if asked you would suppose that the latter was the result of good management while the former was despite the absence of any management whatsoever.

To do the offshore industry justice, the degree of management today is incomparably higher than it was five or ten years ago, and is now way ahead of most other industries. It had to be. The complexity of the technology combined with the limited summer weather window and the confined working space of a platform have forced the industry to sponsor some dramatic managerial techniques based on the computer. And it is these techniques that we shall describe in detail in the course of these chapters. Not because you are about to build an offshore platform, but because these techniques are equally applicable to any industry or commercial enterprise where groups of people interact.

But before we start to go into detail in examining modern industrial or commercial enterprises, it might be illuminating to consider some of the enterprises of the past. After all, *Homo sapiens* has been at it for several millenia now organising large groups of people to build things. What is the difference between the past and the present? What light can such differences shed on the situation today?

When you stand on the parapet of the Great Wall of China and you see the wall stretching to infinity to the east and west along the watershed of some very rugged mountain, you are looking at the biggest project ever mounted by mankind. It was begun over 2,000 years ago. It is 6,000 km long, and apparently is the only evidence of earthly habitation visible from the moon.

Building the Great Wall of China was a project. It involved individual activities such as site surveying, cutting stone, transporting it over the roughest of terrains, putting it in place and reporting back to the Emperor that it was all properly done. It also included obtaining volunteers to carry out the work, training them, housing and feeding them. The resources required to carry out these activities were never very dependable because of the inhospitable climate, abysmal food supply and total lack of regulations about working conditions. Nevertheless the job got finished.

History is full of vast projects

But it wasn't only the Chinese. History is full of vast projects. The Mesopotamians cleared a jungle and established a vast system of irrigation between the Tigris and the Euphrates. The Egyptians built the pyramids and the Ancient Brits Stonehenge. The Incas built a vast network of roadways from the Pacific to the Andes and Offa dug a ditch. In later times Brunel built bridges, Telford dug canals, Clydeside built the Queen Mary and Queen Elizabeth, Eisenhower returned to Europe, and Armstrong landed on the moon 25 years later.

But all of this is only the tip of the iceberg of major projects that people have carried out since long before the dawn of history. None of them used modern management techniques, yet they were very successful. The results of many of them are still around today as eloquent testimony to that success. The Ponte Milvio bridge, built by the Romans, carries traffic over the Tiber still; Italian traffic at that !

If the great projects of the past could be carried out successfully without the use of modern techniques why do we need them today? What's so different between building a pyramid and a power station? Digging irrigation ditches and drilling for oil? Planning cities in the mountains of the Incas and in the deserts of the Saudis?

Well, we can seek a clue by looking at what has happened in other aspects of human endeavour over the ages. Take astronomy. Astronomy existed as a very well understood science, famous for its accuracy, well before Galileo invented the telescope. Biology was a science before the invention of the microscope, physics before the cathode ray tube, and mathematics before the computer. But almost the first time he looked through his telescope, Galileo discovered four of the moons of Jupiter. You can't go back to the naked eye after an eye-opener like that. And when you can see the hairs on the knee of a spider, you will no longer be content with counting butterflies.

Of course, life could have gone on without the invention of instruments. If technical progress had come to an abrupt halt in the twelfth century this planet could have gone on supporting a largish population without life being necessarily nasty, brutish or short. But it didn't and today we wallow in the blessings of technology; the wheel, the pill, the mousetrap and the computer.

The world could have gone on without the computer, and the man in the street wouldn't have noticed much difference. But to some people the computer has made an enormous difference. Today there are several hundred Galileos, who would never dream of going back to the pre-computer days of running a project, because there is a difference. A pyramid is very different to a power station. It is visible. You can see what's going on as you build it. And you notice very easily what needs doing to repair it. For one thing you don't have to shut it down to resharpen the point at the top or replace a block here and there. Building a pyramid is a simple matter of cutting thousands of identical blocks of stone and piling them one upon the other. To find out what's going on, the Pyramid Project Manager merely has to take a walk along the quarry face, and from there along the main drag to the assembly area. If he doesn't like what he sees he simply decimates a slave gang here and there and boosts production to make sure of that target finish.

It's not as easy as that today; modern projects bristle with the invisible. They shriek at you in a thunderous whisper. So you have to look and listen to them in a very different way. And the way you do it is to look at the numbers they produce. By representing all the minute detail in terms of numbers, and putting those numbers into some sort of automatic number-handling device we are able to plan and carry out a project with a degree of control unthinkable to the ancient Mesopotamians - or even the space age managers of the 1960s.

Another important factor that didn't operate even 20 years ago is the tight profit margins that characterise today's business scene. If you have to pay a rate of 15% or 20% on borrowed money you can't afford to have those toilet seats stacked out there in the rain for months while you are still digging the foundations. You can no longer afford sloppy planning or casual implementation.

To give you some idea of the information content of a modern project, a typical offshore field computer system contains some thousand million (10^9) units of information (keyboard characters). This is equivalent to some million sheets of paper, ie a stack of A4 sheets 100 metres high. But not only that; any item of information in the system can be looked at or changed at any time. Imagine trying to find a single number amongst a million sheets of paper and displaying it *within a few seconds!*

But it isn't just changing one number. Any change can lead to a chain-reaction of changes, and this has to be done systematically and quickly. The project manager must know that all the consequences of any change are taken care of without fail. Change is the essence of modern projects.

A project in your company may not be of the same magnitude as an offshore field, but supposing it were only 1%, you would still need 10,000 sheets of paper. Finding a number at random in a book that thick within seconds is still quite a challenge. But if we replace our paper book with an electronic book there is some hope of doing it. And that is what this paper book is all about.

Modern project management techniques put the galaxy of numbers created by the infinite detail of the giant, modern project into clear focus, enabling the project manager to sweep the numerical heavens at the slightest touch to see immediately what is happening there. Try taking it away from him once he's held its power at his fingertips!

Chapter 3

The Basis of Modern Planning

A Mighty Maze But not Without a Plan

Alexander Pope, 1773

When you set out to make or do something of any complexity - which is what this book is about - you need some sort of theoretical basis on which to build the planning and control mechanism. This chapter introduces that theoretical basis, and the following chapters describe the details.

The universe about us is a vast dice, and almost everything that happens in it does so randomly. Almost nothing at all is planned. You can think of the universe as a device for producing temperatures, pressures, masses, distances, forces, accelerations, velocities and compositions of matter, all according to immutable physical laws but in a myriad of combinations. Most of these combinations are lethal. Most of the universe is either too hot or too cold to generate and sustain life. However, out of the chaos at least one set of probabilities has produced an entity capable of order, namely the world we live in. In itself this is a remarkable event, that given enough chaos order can ensue. Not much, I grant you, but some. Even your messy kitchen may contain more order than the entire non-terrestial universe.

But, be that as it may, after some ten thousand million years of randomness a species called *Homo sapiens* has emerged, capable of actually planning its actions. Not all its actions, mark you. Even at this advanced stage most human activity is random, down to the very DNA that defines us. But a growing amount of our activity is planned. It must be so if we are to live together in large numbers, and it behoves us to understand how plans are made and how they can be carried out successfully.

A plan is a structure normally containing time, people, materials, equipment, places, and money which seeks to achieve something. It seeks to produce the most good out of the available resources, within a set of constraints. Unfortunately there are always constraints. Probably if there weren't we wouldn't need to plan.

To produce the most good we need to specify the criteria that a plan must satisfy. What might these be? Here are some possibilities:

1. Maximum profit for the company.
2. Minimum cost of operating a service.
3. Best quality of service within a stated budget.
4. Simplest working rhythm.
5. Maximum deployment of facilities.
6. Most satisfactory human circumstances.
7. Minimum wear and tear, hence maintenance costs.

Usually we encounter a hierarchy of criteria to be satisfied until there are no options left.

Depending on the nature of the problem there will be constraints that the plan will have to satisfy. The following are a few examples:

Physical: One batch of oil cannot pass another in the pipeline. No teacher can be involved in two activities at the same time. Double-decker buses cannot pass under low bridges. You can't put the engines on the wing before the wing is on the body. Only one program can have access to the arithmetic unit at a time.

Legal: No driver may be at the wheel for more than four hours without a meal break. Each child must have a minimum of 35 hours of schooling per week. Paint may not be applied in the absence of toxic removal equipment.

Professional: No mathematics in the afternoon or games in the morning.

Social: Buses may not use the roads adjacent to the hospital.

Functional: The number of people travelling on route 7 between 8.00 am and 9.30 am, Monday to Friday, is 4,350, and they must all have a seat.

Policy: No ship may go beyond 24 months service without a major overhaul.

Safety, Health and Environment (SHE): Fences must be erected around the foundations until the walls are six feet high.

Having defined the problem, the next step in formulating a plan is to determine some *algorithms* or numerical methods that will produce a satisfactory solution. What appropriate method should be used in any particular case? Depending on the nature of the criteria and the constraints, it may be possible to select appropriate algorithms from the list of already existing managerial sciences. But this is not always the case and it may be necessary to perform some research. What is sad to state, however, is that even similar looking situations cannot necessarily use the same algorithms. For example, some pipelines take in all the oil before any is delivered, while others have input and output positions all along the line. Some schools wish to decide precisely which teacher will take which class for which subject, while others are happy to provide lists of alternatives. There is no general-purpose scheduling algorithm. Each case must be considered on its own merits.

At the heart of the matter, however, one can distinguish two distinct types of planning. Let us call them *closed* and *open*. The two fundamental criteria, and they are mutually opposed, are (i) whether a time schedule shall be adhered to and (ii) whether an activity shall be completed. A closed plan, one in which the schedule is paramount, can be thought of as having the appearance of a chess board, with each square a unit of time. A good example is the school timetable. A school timetable contains no provision for actual learning. It merely associates teachers, groups of pupils and classrooms for periods of time. The fourth grade meet in classroom 5 with Mr Smith from 9 til 10, but no learning necessarily takes place. The timetable contains no provision for the fourth grade staying there until they have mastered the French subjunctive. At 10 o'clock the session terminates and the class reassembles for woodwork, all thoughts of the French subjunctive having vanished from their minds.

An open plan is one in which each activity must be completed, even though it takes longer than provided for. An example of open planning is an offshore structure. Indeed, in principle, any physical assembly is of the open type; however, production line methods have made it possible to close most such plans.

All planners aim to create closed plans, but there is rarely a *guarantee* that a physical process can be carried out within a prescribed time period.

This book is concerned with *open* planning, and the basis of open planning consists of two components, the space component and the time component; the thing itself and the business of making it. The space component we call the Work Breakdown Structure (WBS), and the time component, the *network*. These are described in Chapters 4 and 5 respectively. The two together tie into a single planning entity, and everything else we do is built upon them. If you start with this simple idea in mind, all will be crystal clear at all stages, and you will be able to exert complete control as you and your team evolve your particular use of the technology over the years.

Traditionally there are held to be two kinds of people responsible for the two components of planning, the Cost Engineer, whose province is the WBS, and the Planner whose province is the network. This is an unfortunate choice of words because both are planners. Better to call them Cost Engineer and Time Engineer. They are equally important to the planning function, and their responsibilities are inextricably interwoven. So please come to the aid of the party and support my crusade for the sobrique Time Engineer for the keeper of the company's networks.

It may also help to think of the space component as a vertical object, and the time component as a horizontal object, the one tying in with the other along an axis. (This idea is illustrated in Figure 5.3).

Another basic difference is that the WBS can be juggled. Different people view the WBS differently. They have different uses for it, as we shall see in Chapter 4, and it is important that the WBS can be transposed to serve the different needs equally easily and accurately. The network, on the other hand, is fixed in structure. However, the structure may be made to show more or less detail, as circumstances require. And, again, this needs to be done easily and accurately.

Now there is nothing about either a work breakdown structure or a network that necessitates using a computer. It can all be done on paper, but like so many other things these days, it is much faster by computer. Indeed, without the computer the business of detailed planning and management would remain largely of theoretical interest.

So this book is about how to represent the components of a planning system in a computer, and how to use them to help manage projects. We shall do it in logical order, ie the object itself first, and then how to make it, but you may read it in inverse order if you wish. If you want to start with the work breakdown structure just keep on reading. If you want to start with networking, please continue in Chapter 5.

Whichever order you take you will discover that it is very difficult to discuss either in complete isolation. The chapter on the WBS contains inevitable references to networks, and vice-versa.

Chapter 4

Work Breakdown Structures: The Space Component

Work is the Curse of the Drinking Classes

Oscar Wilde

In order to plan the production of any object, from the smallest component to the complete structure, we need to create a picture of it showing its progressive assembly into larger and fewer components, ending
up with the object itself. The structure can be anything. It is the
product (or service) that the project sets out to achieve. It can be a

motor car, aircraft, washing machine or offshore platform, or it can be an annual sales brochure, computer software product or ticketing system. Whatever the object, it will always consist of components, and the components will consist of subcomponents, and so on right down to the nuts and bolts or chapters and paragraphs.

Such a picture we can call a Product Breakdown Structure, and we create it by disassembling it progressively from the whole down to its basic elements. A bicycle, for example, consists of a frame, wheels, mudguards, handlebars, saddle, driving function, gearing and brakes. A wheel, in turn, consists of a tyre, rim, hub, spokes, ball bearings and some nuts, while the driving function consists of pedals, cranks, hub, front cogwheels, chain and back cogwheels. And so on. The weight of the bike is the sum of the weights of its component parts (not forgetting the paint).

The product breakdown structure, then, shows the physical parts of the whole, grouped in a logical and pictorial way.

What it does not show, however, is the work needed to be done to carry out the assembly; attaching the brake cables to the handles, attaching the brake handles to the handlebars, putting the handlebars on the frame, and so on. The product breakdown structure in isolation does not tell us how long it will take to build the bicycle or how much it will cost - the cost being the sum of the prices of the components plus the costs of assembling them.

We need then to draw another picture, identical in form to the product breakdown structure, which we could call the Process Breakdown Structure. To each element in the former there is a corresponding element in the latter. The former contains such information as materials, prices and weights, while the latter contains the times and costs of doing the work.

The two together constitute a picture which is commonly known as the Work Breakdown Structure (WBS). This is an unfortunate term because, of course, it represents more than simply the work. But it has become firmly established in the vocabulary, and is unlikely to disappear. An obvious name for this picture would, of course, be Product and Process Breakdown Structure, but this is too long-winded. An alternative might be Planning Breakdown Structure, but this is unlikely to get much acceptance so I will go along with the crowd and call it WBS throughout the book.

A work breakdown structure, then, is an analysis of the whole in terms of its parts in a nice orderly way. It starts at the top as a single entity and it finishes at the bottom at a level of detail comprising perhaps thousands of entities. The trick is to analyse down to a sensible level, a level that provides a satisfactory basis for the activities of the most detailed associated network. As another illustration let us take the example of an offshore platform.

The entity is the entire platform, an object that consists of a deck and its support. Let these be identified numerically as 1 and 2 respectively. Let us further analyse the deck, component 1. The deck consists of a number of major modules. Let these be numbered thus:

Drilling module	1.1
Process module	1.2
Hotel	1.3
Power generation	1.4

and so on.

Each module consists of contributions from the various engineering disciplines. Let these be numbered:

Mechanical	1
Piping	2
Electrical	3
Instrumentation	4

and so on.

Thus the drilling module mechanical equipment would be coded 1.1.1, process electrical 1.2.3, hotel piping 1.3.2, and so on. The first three levels of the WBS are fairly straightforward. Beyond this at level 4, could come detailed structure, or it could be reporting time-periods (months, say).

Thus drilling mechanical month 1 reporting would be coded 1.1.1.1, process electrical month 6, 1.2.3.6, hotel piping month 4, 1.3.2.4.

On the other hand level 4 might represent packages of work contracted out to other companies.

Pictorially a WBS is represented as illustrated in Figure 4.1. Clearly, the picture is really multidimensional, and the number of boxes multiplies up to something quite large if the detail required is large. Immediately below discipline could come subassemblies such as pumps, generators and lifts, and below that components to be ordered or built.

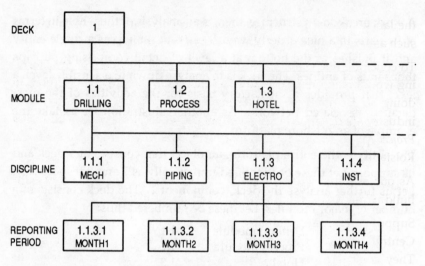

Figure 4.1 WBS: Platform deck

Each WBS is unique. There are general principles and practices, and standards such as drawing numbers and part numbers, but each structure is the result of a new design and the injection of the results of new experience as we learn how to do it better.

Thus a WBS is a special way of representing physical things. Each item is represented by drawings, material codes, parts lists, etc. It has, in itself, nothing to do with time. It says nothing about the actions that have to be carried out to create it, how long they will take, who should do them, how much the work should cost and so on. This is the province of the network.

The important question is how to connect the two. How to dovetail a level of the WBS and its corresponding time component. We shall come back to this in Chapter 5.

While the WBS provides a logical basis for creating the network, an integrated coding scheme between the two provides the basis for cost reporting. Indeed, on the way down a WBS is a physical description mechanism, but on the way up again becomes a cost-accounting mechanism. So, if all work done is reported against network activity, and the activity numbers are automatically tied into the WBS coding, you may *aggregate* data up the WBS and report at any level.

The cost of the entire object, the platform, the motor car, the ticketing system, consists primarily of the cost of the materials and the cost of the labour (but not only those of course; there are lots of minor ones such as services, the cost of borrowed money, rent, etc.)

To conclude this chapter we shall describe the business of transforming work breakdown structures, alluded to in the previous chapter. In doing so we shall use a different example. Details of the offshore industry are described in great detail elsewhere, for example in *Applied Project Management* (Tapir, Trondheim, 1986) by Granli, Hetland and Rolstadaas.

As our example let us revert to the opening chaper and discuss the building industry. What would a building industry WBS look like?

Suppose a building company were engaged in three current projects, Central Hospital, Station Extension and Togetherness Apartments. They could be coded 1, 2 and 3 respectively. At the next level the projects could be subdivided into Land Preparation, 1; Foundations, 2; Walls and Floors, 3; Roof, 4; Exterior Finish, 5; Interior Finish, 6; Inspection, 7. At level 3 would be the trades, Excavation, 1; Concrete, 2; Bricklaying, 3; Carpentry, 4; Glazing, 5; Plumbing, 6; Painting, Papering and Carpeting, 7.

This is enough detail to illustrate the point of transforming a WBS. Let us draw some of it as it currently stands:

LEVEL 1	CENTRAL HOSPITAL		STATION EXTENSION		TOGETHERNESS APARTMENTS		
	1..		2..		3..		
LEVEL 2	LAND PREP	FOUND-ATIONS	WALLS & FLOORS	ROOF	EXT FINISH	INT FINISH	INS-PECT.
	.1.	.2.	.3.	.4.	.5.	.6.	.7.
LEVEL 3	EXCAV-ATION	CONCRETE	BRICK-LAYING	CARP-ENTRY	GLAZING	PLUMBING	PPC
	..1	..2	..3	..4	..5	..6	..7

Thus Central Hospital, Walls and Floors Carpentry would be 1.3.4, while Station Extension, Interior Finish Plumbing would be 2.6.6.

This view of the work breakdown is that of the project manager, and costs would be appropriately summarised up to project level. However, the chief bricklayer has a very different view of things. To him, Bricklaying goes at the top, while the particular project his brickies are currently working on goes at the bottom. To create the chief brick layer's view of the world we simply swap position 1 with position 3 in the coding, producing the following typical picture:

BRICK-LAYING
3

| FOUNDATIONS | | | WALLS & FLOORS | | |
| 3.2 | | | 3.3 | | |

| CENTRAL HOSPITAL | STATION EXTEN | TOGETH APARTM | CENTRAL HOSPITAL | STATION EXTEN | TOGETH APARTM |
| 3.2.1 | 3.2.2 | 3.2.3 | 3.3.1 | 3.3.2 | 3.3.3 |

In this view, costs are collected on the sites and summarised up to the trade level. This allows the chief bricklayer to be responsible for the costs incurred in bricklaying, providing him with an original budget per project and a mechanism for comparing actual expenditures with budget during the life of each project.

This transposition of WBS coding reflects a matrix organisation of the people involved, with a specified team responsible for each project, but with trade departments, or indeed subcontractors, responsible for carrying out the elements of the work.

A good computer system will make it effortless to transform a WBS and report accordingly.

This completes our introduction to work breakdown structures, and in the next chapter we introduce the details of the time component of planning. However, before continuing why not draw a few work breakdown structures of your own to make sure you understand the ideas? Try something easy like a motor car, or if you feel a little adventurous build yourself a hospital.

Chapter 5

Networking: Time Engineering

Sed Fugit Interea, Fugit Inreparabile Tempus
[But Meanwhile Time is Flying, Irretrievable Time Is Flying]

Virgil, 1st. Century B.C.

This chapter and the next describe the very core of project planning, whether you use computers or not. There is no substitute to understanding it. All project discussion takes place in the terminology described here: activity, constraint, early and late starts and finishes, float and critical path. These are the cellular concepts that together make the body of the subject. I have tried to explain it as simply as possible. Although the target audience in this chapter and the next are the project manager and his computer assistant, I don't think at all that it would hurt the general manager to delve into these details. It would help him to know what questions to ask, and how to ask them.

We have described what we mean by a project, with examples from history and everyday life. We have seen how we code and portray the physical attributes of a project, the space component of a plan. We shall now introduce the time component; how to portray the work entailed in implementing the physical attributes.

We said at the end of Chapter 1 that a project consists of a panoply of activities, some in sequence and some in parallel, all carried out in an orderly progression. Let us now draw a picture of this. Let us represent each activity by a box, viz:

```
┌─────────────────────────────┐
│      THIS IS AN ACTIVITY     │
└─────────────────────────────┘
```

and let us denote the orderly progression by means of lines linking the boxes,

```
┌──────────────┐   ┌──────────────┐   ┌──────────────┐
│  ACTIVITY 1  │───│  ACTIVITY 2  │───│  ACTIVITY 3  │
└──────────────┘   └──────────────┘   └──────────────┘
```

This picture states that Activity 2 may start at any time after Activity 1 is finished, and Activity 3 any time after 2 is finished. How long the activities last or how long time-gaps between them might be is a subject for later discussion.

We show concurrent activities by drawing them in parallel, viz:

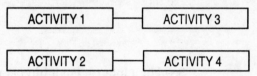

This picture states that Activities 1 and 2 are independent of one another, and may take place concurrently. The same for 3 and 4, where, again, 3 may start any time after 1 has finished and 4 any time after 2 has finished.

In some instances an activity may not start before two or more preceding activities have finished, shown thus:

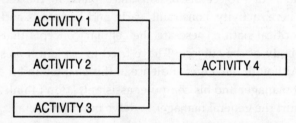

Here Activity 4 cannot start until Activities 1, 2 and 3 have all finished.

In other instances the completion of one activity gives rise to the start of several succeeding activities, thus:

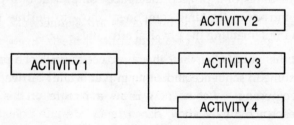

Here Activities 2, 3 and 4 may start when Activity 1 is complete; however they don't necessarily all start simultaneously.

Apart from a few extra details all plans, no matter how complicated or how large, can be described by means of an agglomeration of boxes interconnected by lines denoting their mutual relationships. We call the lines constraints, and we sometimes refer to the activities themselves as nodes. (In Chapter 8 we shall discuss the question of constraints in some detail. But for the purposes of a first reading of this chapter and the next, we will assume a simple definition of constraints as given above.)

We call the entire agglomeration a network. Figure 5.1 shows a small network drawn according to these simple principles.

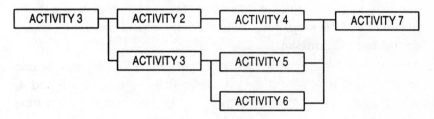

Figure 5.1 A simple network

As a very simple example, you could start your kitchen project as shown in Figure 5.2.

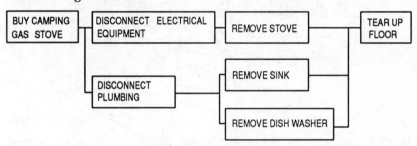

Figure 5.2 An example, using the same network

As an exercise, before reading on, draw your own network representing some simple project such as preparing a meal. Even if you are alone in the kitchen, note that several activities could be carried out concurrently; several saucepans boiling over while you were peeling potatoes or grating the cheese. With several cooks on the job there would be scope for even more concurrency, despite potential broth spoiling.

The ideas we have introduced so far are not new, and you could doubtless find other books introducing networking as the basis for planning. What is usually lacking, however, is any discussion on how to construct a network. This is a lamentable omission because even if you don't use a computer to help you handle the plan, the business of constructing a network is in itself a valuable discipline. Even if you are by yourself, having to think through all the likely happenings before embarking on a course of action will always bring to light things that you would only have otherwise stumbled on in the heat of battle, inevitably causing you a problem. If you don't plan your spaghetti bolognese and ensure the availability of resources as they are required you may find yourself leaping on your bike to buy tomatoes right in the middle of the sauce preparation activity, or end up grating Cheddar instead of Parmesan.

If you don't plan your spaghetti bolognese...

But in the world of industry plans are not normally put together by a single person. In the twelfth century you could know everything, but these days we have the problem of specialisation. Most industrial projects involve contributions from the civil, mechanical, electrical, piping, instrumentation disciplines, and many others, not omitting computing, which is finding its way into everything these days. The basic drawings that define the structure of the job contain contributions from all departments, and therefore so does the plan. So somehow, right at the start (and when is that?), you have the problem of assembling all the planning contributions and creating a single entity out of it. Not easy.

My own first attempt at this was in the early 1970s when the techniques were not in very wide use, and the people involved were not accustomed to talking to one another. I very naively sent out a memo to each discipline leader involved inviting his inputs to the network, expecting to be able to sit down a week later and assemble the jig-saw myself. What replies I received bore no resemblance to one another. It can't be done in isolation. You have to get the entire team into a room and beat the plan out of them. This is how you do it.

You need a windowless room ...

You need a windowless room with two long walls (pictures of the founder removed) covered with large sheets of paper. You need a step-ladder on wheels, a pencil, some felt pens, a Polaroid camera, an energetic secretary, the team and the team leader and a lock on the door. Bread and water until the job is finished.

Only experience can really give you any understanding of the ensuing battle. All I can do is give you some indication. It's somewhat like talking to the blind about colour.

The development of the plan consists of a series of phases as follows.

The Suspicion Phase

When the team is first assembled its members probably haven't met one another before. Moreover, they have very little knowledge of one another's disciplines. The electrical chap couldn't put a shelf up to save his life, and the piping chap couldn't change a light bulb. Yet they have the collective task of creating some single entity, each relying on the others to provide him with their components so that he can get his bit right.

The first hour or two are fraught with suspicion. Each regards his own job as the only important one. The others are there in a support role and don't really understand what it is all about. Anyway, they can't be much good otherwise they'd never have been put on to a project like this.

No one moves. Each eyes the others, and the project leader has a very uncomfortable time getting some energy and direction into the situation.

The piping chap couldn't change
a light bulb

The Confusion Phase

But the project leader isn't there for no reason. He has trod this path before a time or two, and knows how to get things started. The secret is to know that you can start absolutely anywhere. The important thing is to start at all. That's what management is all about. So he points to any member of the team and asks him what his first task will be. After a couple of false starts the selected member will nominate his first activity, and the secretary will draw a box, right in the middle of paper-covered wall 1, standing on the third rung of the step-ladder. In pencil.

The next question is, what needs to be finished before you can start that activity. At first, silence. I mean, what can you expect out of these jokers? Then a trickle, then a stream, then a cascade of rival candidates for the immediately preceding activities. The poor secretary runs up and down the step-ladder, drawing, writing and erasing.

The project leader knows that he needs only three preceding activities, so he selects the most likely from the many suggestions when he's heard enough of the shouting. We can come back to the others later.

Then, which activities can follow? Not so easy. The first contributor doesn't really care, but some of the others will have ideas. Put them down.

Then what activities could take place at the same time as the first selected activity? Another burst of confusion, but out of it will crystallise a set of fairly independent subsets of the network, and those will reflect the physical nature of the product. In aircraft manufacture, for example, body and wing fabrication can take place in parallel until the wing-body join activity, and this will show in the network as two networks coming together towards the right-hand end of the sheet.

This phase will be accompanied by more heat and sound than light, but by the end of it an exhausted secretary will have been able to produce a spaghetti-like picture of about twenty activities, the most lyrical representation of confusion you have ever seen. But better the confusion of the big bang than no creation at all.

Thus endeth the first day, a veritable Belshazzar's feast. If possible, before starting the second have someone redraw the spaghetti in a more lasagne-like way on wall 2 making it easier to handle day 2's continued development of the network. Do this with the felt pen and take a Polaroid picture for the record.

The Educational Phase

By day 2 the team members will know one another a bit, and confidence and understanding will have begun to replace the initial suspicion. Although the picture on the wall will not be easy to understand at a glance, because it has been built up detail by detail by the team, the team will understand it. But let me repeat, it will help a lot if someone could volunteer to stay behind to redraw the network in a more orderly form, trying to minimise the routes taken by the constraints. This makes it possible to increase the number of activities and constraints on day 2 without making the picture totally hopeless.

As the picture develops, more and more descriptive information will be written on it. As this happens try to make it as structured as possible. Colour code the activity boxes according to discipline; there may be more than one discipline involved in a single activity. Number the activities in some semblance of order; you will need these numbers later. Use short versions of the activity descriptions on the picture itself, while the discipline leaders write full versions on their note pads. Where the constraint lines are too long, cut them short and use Greek letters for indicating the connections. And make frequent use of the Polaroid. Make it easy to reduce the detail if you find you've gone too far.

Day 2 will produce three times as many activities as day 1, bringing the total up to eighty, and this is enough for the wall version of any network. During the day mutual understanding and agreement will accelerate, and from it will already emerge an understanding of the project at a level of detail *unprecedented by any previous discussion.* Hitherto hidden problems will emerge; research items where the current technology isn't up to requirement; doubts perhaps about the market; estimates of budget much higher than initially thought.

Note that so far we haven't made any use of a computer. All we are doing is readying ourselves to do so. This is a very interesting parenthetical point. During the build-up of the network the paper on the wall takes on a life of its own and begins to dominate the proceedings. The wall makes discoveries. It tells us things. It unites us in attacking it. The eventual use of a computer acts as a catalyst to our ways of doing things, and during this stage appears through its surrogate, the wall.

The Subnet Phase

If day 2 finishes with a single network of eighty, or at most a hundred activities and their accompanying web of constraints you have done very well. You might find it taking closer to a week to get that far.

At that level of detail select those activities which contain the most work and expand them, one by one, into individual networks in their own right on wall 2. Out of a hundred you might find ten that need this extra level of detail. We call these objects *subnets*. You might even find that an occasional activity in a subnet needs yet a further level of detail.

When should this process finish? Well, no network should contain more than about 100 activities before being subject to subnetting, and a good criterion to apply would be that the resultant effort in each lowest level activity should be about the same. But we haven't talked about effort yet, so we are jumping the gun a bit here.

The Computer Phase

When one wall has been covered in network, and the other in subnets; when your team is exhausted, the step-ladder bent hopelessly out of shape and your secretary has resigned for the fifth time this week you stop. You've gone far enough. You've reached the stage where it's better to use a computer than carry on with the people.

We shall explain how the computer does it later on. All we need say at this point is that every activity has an identifying number, and each constraint is defined by the numbers of the activities at its start and end points. It is therefore an easy matter to enter a numerical description of the network into the computer, allowing the computer to redraw the network in a neat orderly way, converting the spaghetti into lasagne.

The species Homo sapiens *has survived mainly because of its optimism*

The Time Estimate Phase

When the team has gone as far as it can to creating the geometry of the network, it must then make the first tentative step towards turning it into a plan; it must estimate the time required for each activity. Another round of argument. The problem here lies deep in the human psyche. The species *Homo sapiens* has survived mainly because of its optimism. Rabbits go on eating grass only moments after they have run away from the fox, and are apparently then oblivious of the fox's existence. Human beings are much the same. Were we to allow our impressions of reality to accumulate in our memories we would have become extinct aeons ago from universal heart failure. History is the history of disaster, and yet we get up each morning and go whistling down the road as though nothing could possibly happen.

While it is our optimism that goads us on to success, it is the same optimism that sows the seeds of failure when it comes to trying to plan that success. Estimating involves memory. Our picture of the future is based on what we remember of the past. But we only remember the good things, and it seems but yesterday - and so on.

History is the history of disaster

Estimating unaided by a comprehensive diary is a recipe for disaster and a source of bitter dispute. But better the dispute than a docile acceptance of someone's first guess just because he's got the loudest voice or he's the boss or whatever. In Chapter 10 we'll talk about experience databases, but there's lots to be done before we can get that far. In the meantime we'll do the best with what we've got, the human memory aided perhaps by some numbers gleaned from similar under-takings, unaccountably retained in someone's filing system.

The time units must be appropriate to the duration of the project. A strategic plan extending over months would use days, while a finely tuned plan of less than a month would probably use hours.

The duration estimate for each activity is written on the box alongside the activity number and description.

The work that is done to carry out the assembly of each element of a WBS is plannable via a piece of network. Since most of the work is done at the lowest level of the WBS, the major network exists at that level, and Figure 5.3 is an attempt at depicting the fundamental rela-relationship between the two. As we said earlier, we may think of the

WBS as a vertical object, and the network as horizontal. This is illustrated in Figure 5.3.

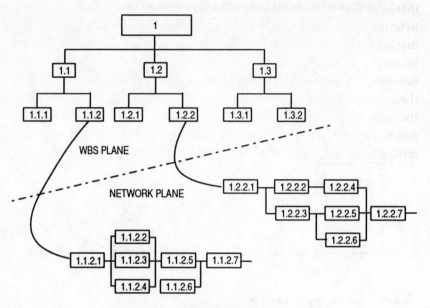

Figure 5.3 A WBS tied to a network

Here we have carried the WBS coding over to the network coding by adding a further digit, so that any particular network activity or group of activities can be automatically identified with its WBS element.

In principle there are networks at every level, drawn in increasing simplicity as we move up. However, in practice we are usually able to mesh everything into a single network.

This is perhaps a rather simplistic picture. In actual practice, especially in large and complicated structures, it may not be easy to establish a strict one-to-one correspondence, but it is a goal well worth trying for as the plan is built up.

Having described the two basic structures of project planning I will finish this chapter with an introductory word about the use of computers. In all that follows there is an underlying assumption that you will be using a computer of some sort to handle the ideas in practice. And as I am sure you are well aware, computer technology has always been ahead of our ability to use it adequately. The newest hardware and software is always more powerful than what we happen to have on our own desk at any point in time. Whatever system you happen to be using, there will always be a new one on someone's shelf that seems to do the job better. This is also true with writing books. It would therefore be a futile exercise to try to prescribe a system in these pages in terms of any particular technology. Something new would be on the market before the ink was dry. Suffice it to say that you should always be on the lookout for systems that allow you to work as close to the network as possible during the planning (and replanning) phase. It is the network that is the planner's principle computing object. While in the network you need simple and responsive recourse to its associated functions, be it via menus, windows, icons, mouses or ying tong iddle ipos, whatever the industry happens to be providing at the time.

Chapter 6

Analysing Networks

Sweet Analytics, 'Tis Thou Hast Ravished Me

Christopher Marlowe, 1588

Even if you were to leave it at that, and content yourself with creating a plan so that each member of the team knew what was expected of him and how his work was to relate to that of the others, you would be way ahead of most people. You would have a vehicle for managing the project; a representation of the project to use as a goad to urge the team to fulfil its obligations.

But you can do much more than that. A network contains a lot of information in its own right and can be harnessed to a lot more information supplied to it.

The primary set of information is obtained by carrying out an *analysis* of the network. Analysis is a very simple process requiring only the ability to add and subtract, and to do so in a methodical way.

Let us now draw the example network, Figure 6.1, in a little more detail. We will explain the meaning of the small squares as we go along.

For simplicity each activity is labelled with a number, A1, A2 and so on, instead of the sort of coding that we encounter in real life as illustrated in Figure 6.2 on page 44, and in the top left-hand corner of each large square we have already written the duration DU. The units can be anything, hours, days, weeks or months.

We now wish to *analyse* the network, that is to say to find out when each activity can start and finish, plus some other very interesting additional information. In order to do so please copy the network on to a separate sheet of paper and follow the steps with pencil (and eraser!). Only by doing it yourself will you really understand it, and discover how easy it is to handle a network.

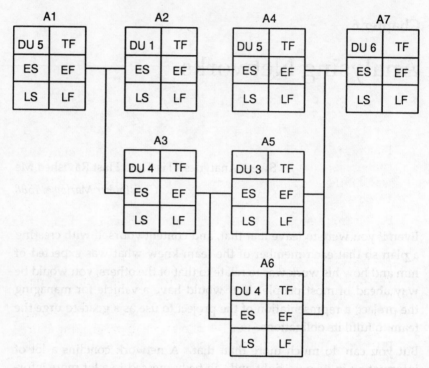

Figure 6.1 The network of Figure 5.1 showing more detail

The steps are as follows:

1. *The forward pass*

   We start by examining each activity in turn to determine how early it can start and finish. We do this in strict order left to right.

   In each activity box there is a box labelled ES, early start, and one labelled EF, early finish. Let us say that activity A1 starts at time zero. Write a zero in ES box of A1. The early finish of A1 is clearly 5.

   For every activity, EF = ES+DU. Please satisfy yourself that this is so.

   Now the earliest that A2 can start is the instant A1 has finished, ie the ES of A2 = the EF of A1. Thus the ES of A2 = 5. Similarly the ES of A3 = 5. Please enter these numbers in the appropriate boxes.

   We can now proceed to the next column of activities.

A4: ES = A2's EF = 6
     EF = 6 + 5 = 11

A5: ES = A3's EF = 9
     EF = 9 + 3 = 12

A6: ES = A3's EF = 9
     EF = 9 + 4 = 13

Finally we come to A7. What is A7's earliest possible start? A7 cannot start until *all* of its predecessors have finished. It must wait for the *latest* of predecessors, ie A6, where the early finish is 13. So A7's ES = 13, and its EF = 13 + 6 = 19.

So the entire project takes 19 units, and we have completed the forward pass.

2. *The backward pass*

We now examine each activity in turn starting from A7 and moving to the left, to determine the *latest* allowable start and finish, noting that for each activity LF (late finish) = LS (late start) + DU, ie LS = LF - DU. Since we don't wish to prolong the entire project, by definition A7's late finish, LF, equals its EF, 19, while its late start, LS, equals its ES, 13.

Think carefully

Now examine A4. Its latest possible finish must equal A7's LS, 13, and its LS = LF - DU = 13-5 = 8. The next three activities are as follows:

A5: LF = A7's LS = 13
     LS = 13 - 3 = 10

A6: LF = A7's LS = 13

$$LS = 13 - 4 = 9$$

A2: $LF = A4's\ LS = 8$
             $LS = 8 - 1 = 7$

Now the catchy one. Think carefully. As far as A5 is concerned, A3 can finish at time 10. But if it did, A6 would be delayed because its latest start is 9. Therefore A3's LF must be 9, and its $LS\ 9 - 4 = 5$.

We have the same problem with A1, its LF must be A3's LS, 5, and not A2's, which is 7. And A1's $LS = 5 - 5 = 0$, exactly what you would expect. If it weren't you would have made a mistake somewhere.

We have now determined all the latest starts and finishes, and have completed the backward pass. But before continuing make absolutely sure that you understand the process, and that your results agree with mine. It is the core of networking. The core of time engineering. The core of planning. The core of project control.

When printing reports you may, if you wish, call EF "MAY START" and LF "MUST FINISH".

3. *The critical path*

We now turn our attention to the last box in each activity, TF; total float. We define the total float of each activity to be the difference between its LS and its ES.

In our example:

A1:	$TF = 0 - 0 = 0$	A5:	$TF = 10 - 9 = 1$
A2:	$TF = 7 - 5 = 2$	A6:	$TF = 9 - 9 = 0$
A3:	$TF = 5 - 5 = 0$	A7:	$TF = 13 - 13 = 0$
A4:	$TF = 8 - 6 = 2$		

Write these numbers in the appropriate boxes to complete your picture.

The total float of an activity is the amount of time it can be delayed beyond its earliest possible start without delaying the total project. Thus we see that A2 and A4 may be delayed two time units, and A5 one, without delaying A7. On the other hand, the sequence of activities A1, A3, A6 and A7 have total floats of zero. None of these activities can be delayed without delaying the entire project, and we call this sequence the *critical path* through the network.

Analysing a network will always yield a critical path, and it is this sequence of activities that the project manager must pay most attention to during the life of the project. He can allow delays in other paths (up to the limit of their total float) but not in the critical path.

4. *Converting to dates*

Having obtained points in time, 0,1,2, etc., the final stage is to convert them to actual days or hours. In Chapter 7 we describe the nature of a calendar in detail, but for present purposes we can say that the computer system contains a calendar program containing information about workable days and hours, holidays etc. As an example let us suppose that the time unit is a day, and that the worked shift is from 9 til 5. Then the first activity in a network might start at 9 am on a Monday, ie time zero = 9 am. Then time 1 would be both 5 pm Monday *and* 9 am Tuesday. As far as the system is concerned work takes place continuously and the unworked shifts are ignored. Point 5 would be both 5 pm Friday and 9 am Monday. And so on.

If the units were hours the system would convert points in time to hours in a day in a similar way.

At this point you can leave this chapter and continue with the next. The remainder is only a more detailed treatment of the foregoing. By now you have encountered the essential items.

I hope you will agree at this stage that analysing a network yields some very useful information. Even though a network may consist of a large number of activities of widely varying durations, it is easily possible to determine the length of its combined duration. And it tells you where to concentrate your managerial attention. How often does that happen to you in life?

I hope also that you had no problem following the steps. But to make sure, let's do it twice more, varying the network a little and observing the result. Let us say that we wish to enter an extra activity, A8. It is dependent on A5 and A6 and has a duration of 4. The network will look as shown in Figure 6.2 on page 44.

Copy it down and carry out an analysis; first a forward pass, A1 to A7, and then a backward pass, A7 to A1. Finally the critical path. As you do it you evolve a nice working rhythm. That in turn helps you remember the definitions.

Well, what happened? If your solution agrees with mine the whole project has been delayed by 4 units to time 23; A8 lies smack bang on the critical path, and A2's and A4's total floats have increased to 6. We couldn't have made a worse mess of things. Good thing we had the network to help us test the effect of the placing of A8.

To try to improve matters, let's move A8 off the critical path and place it between A4 and A7 (supposing that it is possible technically to do so). The network will now look as shown in Figure 6.3.

Again, carry out an analysis and see how much we have been able to improve matters. After a third go I'm sure you'll feel able to tackle any network they place before you provided it isn't too big. How many activities do you think you could manage in an hour? And get the right answers? Fifty perhaps?

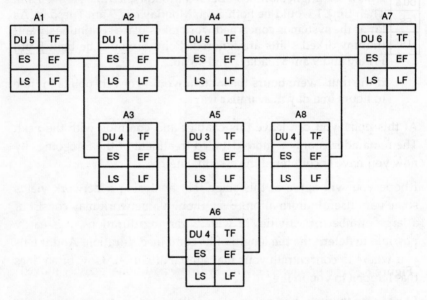

Figure 6.2 The previous network with one additional activity

What answers did you get this time? According to my calculations the project finish has dropped back to 21. But the critical path has jumped to the sequence A1, A2, A4, A8, A7. A2 and A4 have lost their total float, while A5's has increased to 3, and A3 and A6 have acquired a float of 2.

What we have done here is buy as much time as we can with the maximum total float at our disposal, ie 2, minimising the total delay. We have achieved this by placing the intruder on the path of maximum float.

This is almost all there is to it, but not quite. In addition to the durations of the activities themselves we are allowed to place time delays on the *constraints*. The traditional example of this is allowing three days for the cement to dry before the next activity can start. To carry out the analysis simply add the delay to the following duration.

What would be the result of putting a time delay of 6 units on the constraint between A3 and A5? The sequence A1, A3, A5, A7 would go critical. The project would end at time 24. A2, A4 and A8 would have a total float of 3, and A6 a total float of 5. Do you agree?

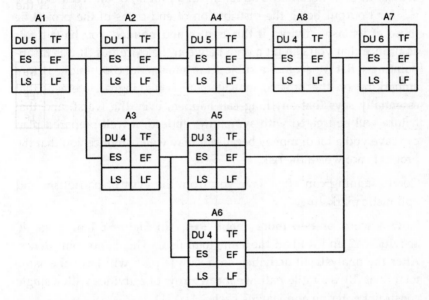

Figure 6.3 The previous network with the additional activity moved

But what would happen if you had a time delay of only 3 between A3 and A5? A3 and A5 would go critical making *two* critical paths in the network, while A6's total float would be 2.

The next step in order of complication is what to do about activities whose duration you cannot reasonably be sure of. This is the development project problem. You might be lucky first time in a piece of development work, but you might not. You might have to redesign and carry out an activity a second time and a third. You might be chasing rainbows. Does this mean you can't plan? Or does it mean that the need for planning is more vital than ever? Development projects are notoriously late, and designers are scared stiff to publish plans.

That's very understandable. But a well-structured published and explained plan brings the parent organisation on to the punch.

The way to do this is to subject the network to a Monte Carlo statistical analysis. This is done in the following way. Each uncertain activity is given two limiting durations, an optimistic and a pessimistic, together with a distribution between the two (rectangular, Gaussian etc., whichever is appropriate). The analysis routine is then set to run a thousand times, say, generating a random value for each uncertain activity at each iteration. You let it run all night, or all weekend, the essential output being the distribution of end dates of the project, ie those of its last activity. If this is nice and pointed you have a fair assurance that you can hit a date between the extremes. If it is disappointingly flat it becomes a subject for managerial discussion. Before embarking on the project, management is signing a statement that essentially says that anything can happen, even the worst, and that failure will be treated with sympathy. Indeed, a well-prepared plan can save you a lot of money because it may well convince you that the project is not worth the risk.

Good planning can often save you from the evils of patriotism and optimistic marketing.

Now a word or two more about float. In Figure 6.1 on page 40 activities A2 and A4 had the same total float. This is no coincidence. After the analysis all activities on a simple path will have the same total float. By a simple path we mean a row of activities with a single constraint entering and leaving each.

In our example if A2 is delayed, A4 will lose some float. Indeed the amount it loses will equal precisely the delay in A2. Try a few examples to convince yourself of this. In other words the total float of A2 and A4 isn't "owned" by the activities themselves, but is a property of the entire path. In the extreme case, if A2 starts at its LS, A4 will have a TF of zero, ie will be critical.

So total is what it says, total. It is the entire float available to all the activities comprising a particular simple path. Or you can say it is the float that an activity owns provided its predecessor starts at ES and its successor at LS.

But there are other species of float. They are smaller but progressively more "private". As an illustration of these let us rearrange Figure 6.2

on page 44 a bit and increase the duration of A4 to 7, as visualized in Figure 6.4.

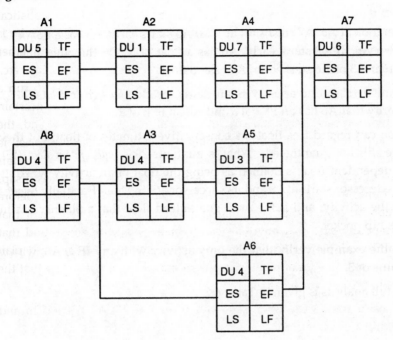

Figure 6.4 A rearrangement of the network in Figure 6.2

The analysis gives Table 6.1.

Table 6.1						
ACT	DU	ES	EF	LS	LF	TF
A1	5	0	5	0	5	0
A2	1	5	6	5	6	0
A3	4	4	8	6	10	2
A4	7	6	13	6	13	0
A5	3	8	11	10	13	2
A6	4	4	8	9	13	5
A7	6	13	19	13	19	0
A8	4	0	4	2	6	2

Thus the critical path is A1, A2, A4, A7. Now let us examine the float of each activity when both its predecessor and successor start at their ES. This reduced float we call *free float early* (FFE). The only candidates for an FFE are, of course, A3, A5, A6 and A8. In the case of A3 and A8, if A5 starts early, A3 and A8 will be forced to start early and have no float.

But look at A5. A7 *must* start at 13. If A3 starts early, A5 has a float of 2. Also A6. If A8 starts early, A6 has a float of 5. On the other hand if either A3 or A6 start early, A8 has no float.

Similar reasoning appl.. to late starts, producing *free float late* (FFL). Verify that A6 has an FF. of and A8 an FFL of 2.

You can regard free floats as conservative estimates of float, but they are still not guaranteed. What is guaranteed is *independent float* (IF). Independent float is defined as being the float of an activity when its predecessor starts at LS and its successor at ES. Thus IF actually *belongs* to the activity, and is the most guaranteed float that a planner has in his hip pocket.

In the example verify that the only activity with any IF is A6, with a value of 3.

A full analysis is given in Table 6.2.

Table 6.2									
ACT	DU	ES	EF	LS	LF	TF	FFE	FFL	IF
A1	5	0	5	0	5	0	0	0	0
A2	1	5	6	5	6	0	0	0	0
A3	4	4	8	6	10	2	0	0	0
A4	7	6	13	6	13	0	0	0	0
A5	3	8	11	0	13	2	2	0	0
A6	4	4	8	9	13	5	5	3	3
A7	6	13	19	13	19	0	0	0	0
A8	4	0	4	2	6	2	0	2	0

To conclude the discussion on float, it is possible to impose upon a network target dates independent of the natural analysed dates. The planner may require that come what may an activity must be complete by a certain date. A system will allow him to enter a so-called *target finish*, and if this is earlier than the analysed early finish (ie in theory the date cannot be achieved) the difference between the dates will be displayed as *negative float*. The converse is a *target start*.

If a target start is later than the analysed late start the difference will be added to the natural float, and this can result in a network losing its critical path altogether.

Advice is to impose dates as little as possible. It is difficult enough to achieve natural dates. To require that a plan finishes earlier than the earliest theoretically possible is a recipe for disaster.

To complete this chapter mention should be made of a special kind of activity called a *hammock*. It is an "inactive" activity, a dummy for measuring the time taken between any two points in the network. The DU of a dummy is output from the analysis, not input to it. The two points are generally the start and finish of a section of network that has had some special meaning to the planner, and although he has the start and finish dates, and the elapsed time, he is interested in the number of working days between the two. This is what the hammock provides.

Figure 6.5 shows a hammock strung across a section of network. In this example it will measure the elapsed time in working days from the first early start to the last early finish of the five activities.

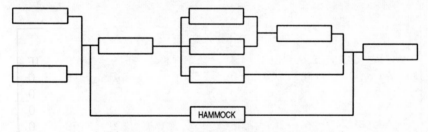

Figure 6.5 An example of a hammock

This completes our introduction to network analysis. However, there is a little more to it than that. We have made it deliberately simple to start with, but by the time you have completed Chapter 8 you should be able to handle any network that presents itself. The next step is to extend the resources required beyond that of time - so far the only resource we have dealt with.

Chapter 7

Scheduling

I Will Give Out Diverse Schedules

Shakespeare, Twelfth Night

An analysed network is a plan based on one resource - time. Time is the only element common to all activities and is therefore the only resource that could possibly be included in the first version of any plan.

After time can come anything: people, premises, equipment, materials, money, whatever resources you need to carry out that activity.

The next step then is to produce a plan based on all the resources. This requires a systematic statement of what resources are needed for each activity, and what resources are available during the life of the project. In turn this reveals the need for calendars, especially where people are concerned.

Although we haven't spoken about computers yet, in any detail, we can now start to prepare for this by beginning to use codes as we talk about resources and calendars. In actual practice the only way to create a schedule based on a network is to use a computer because of the amount of systematic searching and matching needed to assign the resources to the activities. I am sure that the detail here and in the next chapter will bemuse most general managers, and it can be safely left to the project manager and his computer man.

Let us start with calendars. Basically a computer system needs to contain a single complete calendar starting somewhere historical, say 1st January 1990, with all the days of the week coded in, stretching on to some date far out in the future, eg 31st December 1999. Call this calendar zero.

On this we can build any number of calendars suitable for our purposes. A first set might be religious calendars. A Christian calendar would block out all Saturdays and Sundays, Christmas Day and New Year's Day, together with a complicated arrangement of Good Fridays and Easter Days. A Muslim calendar would presumably allow work at Christmas but would block out Ramadan. It would block out Fridays but presumably allow work at the weekends. The Jews and Buddhists have their own New Years, while presumably the atheists work all the time. Let the religious calendars be numbered 1 to 5.

Then come the national calendars. Each country has its own set of holidays. In Norway the month of May is more or less a write-off.

By now we could have quite a comprehensive set of standard calendars, but in addition we have the ability to create our own local calendars. For example we may have to work a six-day week over a particular period. Also each individual has his own vacation if we are working on an individual level. On the other hand equipment, such as cranes, may be available continuously.

MAi

...the month of May is more or less a write-off

Any computer system must have the ability to specify any calendar the user wishes, and to be able to specify the start and end dates of the availability of any resource, together with its code. Here are some examples:

Welders:

```
code W: availability on calendar 7
            23 from  1-FEB-91 to   9-MAY-91
            25 from 10-MAY-91 to 11-AUG-91
            14 from 12-AUG-91 to 14-SEP-91
```

George Crudworthy:

```
code GC: availability on calendar 4
             holiday from 17-JUL-91 to 3-AUG-91
```

Cranes:

```
code C: availability on calendar 0
             4 from 1-JAN-91
```

Having entered the availability of each resource over the expected period of the project we may then enter its requirement by activity. Some examples:

Activity A27   DIG FOUNDATIONS
        1   excavator:code E
        1   driver:code ED

Activity A33   POUR CEMENT
        1   mixer:code MX
        1   operator:code MXOP
        1   wheelbarrow:code WB
      2.7   tons cement:code CEM
        2   navvies:code NAV

Activity A42   INSTALL COMPRESSOR
        1   compressor:code COM
        1   crane:code CRN
        1   driver:code CD
        3   electricians:code ELEC
        2   plumbers:code PLUM
        4   mechanics:code MECH

This can be quite a lengthy business but the payoff is well worth the effort as we shall see. When finished we are then in a position to run the first schedule. Fundamentally there are two types of schedule. We call them *time-limited* and *resource-limited*.

Time-limited Scheduling

Time-limited scheduling is a process by which we assign resources to activities where they are available, but we maintain the dates obtained during the analysis, and where resources are unavailable we merely report the matter. We say the resources are in *overload*.

The first step is to assign resources to all the critical activities, to the extent they are available, and subtract them from the availabilities. Possible overload is the signal for acquiring more people, equipment or materials in order to keep to the scheduled dates.

Having dealt with the critical activities we can then deal with the non-critical. But this is easier said than done. Critical activities have no float therefore there are no options to pursue. The non-critical activities can be placed anywhere between early start and late start, a simple statement but with very complicated consequences. There are many ways of adjusting the arrangement of activity starts, with corresponding resource allocations. Each pattern of starts produces a unique arrangement of possible overloads and underloads, and finding some kind of optimum is by far the biggest problem to be solved in any planning system. Indeed it is one of the biggest problems we use computers for.

Probably today very few users of planning systems are aware of the underlying difficulties, and are happy enough to get a schedule at all. And perhaps this is as it should be. We should be able to rely on the power of the computer to find its way through the vast number of possible patterns that a combinatorial problem presents, and find a good solution. However, the reader who really wants to do his homework should read *Activity Networks* by S. Elmaghraby (Wiley, NY, 1977).

Furthermore the discerning computer user may wish to compare the efficacy of rival solutions. The following describes some of the considerations the planner in combination with the system is confronted with.

1. *Speed vs exhaustiveness*

   The fundamental fact of life is that the large number of possible combinations of overload and underload will take an appreciable amount of time to evaluate on any computer, however fast.

But in the early stages of creating a plan, at least, the planner will want to move quickly. Time for refinement when he has a better idea of what he's doing.

The rest of the items on this list are all manifestations of this underlying problem.

2. *Defining an optimum*

    If we ask the computer to find us an optimum plan we must tell it what we mean by optimum. Do we mean for example:

    • earliest possible completion regardless of cost

    • cheapest completion regardless of time

    • minimum variation of resource loadings from period to period

    • minimum hiring-in of particular resources (eg welders)

    • maximum scheduling at Early Start to play for safety

    or -

    maximum scheduling at Late Start to delay expenditure as much as possible?

3. *Minimising cost*

    If an activity requires several resources, and there is no point of no-overload in one or another resource, how do we decide which is the best possible schedule?

    There may be one position of minimum wheelbarrows and another of minimum welders. Without converting resources to actual costs there is really no way of computing a minimum.

    In most computer planning systems, however, the costs of resources are not taken into consideration at the planning stage. These usually come in later on as they are actually incurred. Nevertheless, minimising cost at the planning stage is certainly feasible provided the system contains a cost-calculation feature. Such a feature would need to know the unit costs of different categories of people, in particular overtime rates, the premium costs of early delivery of materials, the costs of storage of bulk materials, and could even take into consideration the cost of money.

    If there is no computer system today that does this it is because it would cost a lot to do it properly, and would take a long time to run. The payoff, however, might well be worth it.

4. *Fast scheduling*

    A fast scheduler is one that, having assigned a resource to an activity over a period of time, sticks to the decision. And it does so without looking ahead and analysing the consequences of its actions. It moves from activity to activity in some way, making the best choice right now, but never going back to find out whether it could have made a better one by rearranging its predecessors. This is called the "greedy" method in the trade. Greedy scheduling can be a one-way street to a poor schedule, but it does not take much computer time, and is certainly acceptable in the very approximate early stages.

5. *Single-resource scheduling*

    One problem a scheduler has is that of dealing with several, and therefore possibly conflicting, resources. The difficulty of scheduling rises very steeply with the number of resources. The fewer the better, and of course if there is only one type of resource throughout the entire schedule, the problem is almost as simple as the initial time analysis.

6. *Weighted resources*

    There is no point in delaying an activity involving Einstein and a wheelbarrow if all we have to do is buy an extra wheelbarrow. A compromise between full cost-analysis scheduling and single-resource scheduling is to weight the resources in order of cost, availability, flexibility etc. The computer takes each in turn and "spends" float on achieving an optimum within progressively reduced limits until there is no float left.

7. *Criticality*

    Off the critical path there is a hierarchy of paths of different total float. Some activities may be of short duration and long float, others of long duration and short float. How realistic are the estimates of duration? How many activities could really go critical in the heat of battle? A scheduling algorithm could take this question into consideration and treat activities of relatively short total float as already critical, thus reducing the computing time and making a more conservative schedule.

These factors are by no means a complete description of the time-limited scheduling problem and its solutions. However they do give some indication of its complexity, and some clues about what to look for in a computer solution. The best advice that can be proferred is to find a system that gives the planner a fair amount of control. A planner should be able to decide for himself how refined he wants the schedule. Typically he would like fast and therefore perhaps crude early versions, followed eventually by a very refined overnight run taking advantage of every feature the system can allow.

Resource-limited Scheduling

Resource-limited scheduling is a process by which we assign resources to activities where they are available, and never go into overload. Thus we allow activities to be delayed until a time at which resources are available, even if this means delaying beyond Late Start. Activities which were uncritical after the analysis phase can become critical after resource-limited scheduling. Thus the critical path can be radically altered by the unavailability of resources, which de facto take priority over the topology of the network.

This makes resource-limited scheduling much more difficult than time-limited. You no longer have the life-line of the analysed critical path to cling to. In time-limited scheduling the critical path stays critical, and therefore gives you a piece of skeleton on which to hang the non-critical activities. When you bump up against Late Start in your search for resources, you simply surrender and shout out "overload". Not so with resource-limited scheduling.

In other words resource-limited has far more degrees of freedom than time-limited, and it is much less obvious how to obtain a good schedule. The numbers of possible combinations are often very high.

Beyond that, what applies to the non-critical activities in time-limited scheduling applies also in resource- limited scheduling. Remember always that no computer system can be made omniscient. You, the user, will always know more about the project than you can tell the computer. Using it is always a trade-off between delegating as much of the effort as possible to the high-speed number-cruncher, and reserving enough for yourself to enable you to override the computer where necessary.

This is probably sufficient to indicate that there are many ways of producing a schedule, and you should find a system that suits your needs. The important point to be made is that scheduling is a combinatorial problem. That is, it involves enormous amounts of possibilities, and even on a computer it can take appreciable time. A schedule is not unique, and we are never satisfied with what the computer produces, but better to let the computer take that time, crunch those numbers, examine those combinations, and produce something that we can fine-tune ourselves rather than lurch from crisis to unplanned crisis as we've been doing in the past.

Chapter 8

Constraints

And Nat to Been Constrayned

Chaucer, The Franklin's Tale

Having discussed the basic problems of scheduling, and some of the solutions, we now pick up the question of constraints. We briefly defined constraints as lines joining the activities for timing purposes. There is actually more to it than that, and there are often more problems than there are solutions.

We begin by examining the activity constraints. Initially we saw that a time constraint indicated that the following activity could not start before the preceding activity had finished, and we drew it thus:

We call this a *finish-to-start* constraint, FS. This is the most common type of constraint. Indeed, many networks contain only this type.

Consider now the case of two activities which can take place in parallel, one following the other with perhaps a slight delay. As an example take the activities constructing a fence and painting it. If the fence takes any substantial time to erect there would be no point in waiting until it was finished before starting the painting. Provided the painter waited a while, say a day, the carpenter could work without getting paint down his neck, but both could work at the same time.

There are two possible situations, either the painting takes more time than the construction or less.

If the painting takes the longer time we can use a *start-to-start* (SS) constraint with a one day delay, shown thus:

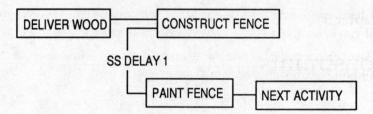

A start-to-start constraint allows the successor to start after the predecessor has started rather than wait for it to finish. In this case we know that the successor will finish last, so we continue the network from it, probably with an ordinary finish-to-start.

If the painting takes the longer time ...

However, if the construction takes the longer time we can use a *finish-to-finish* (FF) constraint, again with a one day delay, shown thus:

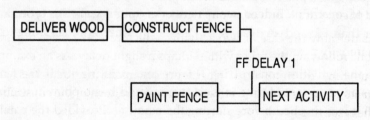

A finish-to-finish constraint forces the successor to finish after the predecessor has finished, but allows it to start some time after the predecessor has started. By definition the successor finishes last, so we continue the network from it, again almost certainly with a finish-to-start.

And here's an exercise for the student; which constraint would you use if you knew that both activities would take exactly the same time?

The last type of constraint, the only combination of F and S left, is the start-to-finish constraint, SF, drawn as follows:

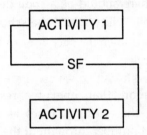

This one needs a little thinking. Activity 2 cannot be said to be finished before Activity 1 has started. For example, a site uses its own power generator until the mains electricity has been coupled. Operating the generator cannot *finish* until the mains supply has *started*. This could be shown as follows:

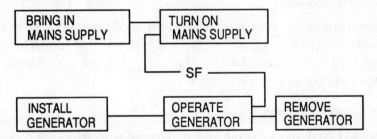

This completes the *geometry* of the network. At this point it might be a good idea to draw one or two networks of your own with constraints other than FS, and analyse them. You'll find there's much more to it than initially meets the eye, so be systematic.

Let us now examine what might go on inside the activities, the *dynamics* of the network, starting with considerations of the constraints on the resources:

The Shovel-Leaning Problem

You can only have one dentist struggling at the mouth of a patient. You can't have more than two sailors in a small dinghy. On the other hand the Emperor of China had an unlimited number of stone-cutters on the Great Wall. Clearly there are physical constraints on the applicability of human resources, despite their availability, and I am sure you have observed road-workers faced with this problem. You will have seen one actually doing something, his colleagues contemplating the quality of his work, perhaps proferring advice or even offering words of encouragement.

In a computer system there should be a code denoting possible constraints on resource applicability which the scheduler must take into consideration.

Variability

In those cases where more than one of a resource type may be allocated to an activity the question arises as to whether you are restricted to using a fixed number throughout the life of the activity, or may use a variable number, depending on availability. You may perhaps use as many painters as you can get hold of, for example, but for installing the cables in the wall cavities you must have two electricians but cannot use three. So the number of painters assigned might vary each period, depending on availability, while the number of electricians is constant.

Again, constraints on the level of allocated resources need to be coded activity-by-activity. However, the less you use this constraint the easier you will make it for the scheduling program, and the better overall loading level you will achieve.

The Cockpit Problem

You can't have more than three maintenance workers in the cockpit. From the point of view of working space, a location can resemble a chair (a single person), a wall (a row of people), a field (a spread of people) or a skyscraper (a heap of people). Each activity will take place in some physical location and should be coded as to the space allowable for people to work in it.

Teams

A painter may not be allowed to pick up a hammer, while a plumber may not be allowed to replace a broken window with a piece of cardboard. It was not like this during man's evolution to his present state, but it is so today in many countries. Nevertheless, although we think of the different trades as independent, and belonging to different unions, they sometimes have to be allocated to activities in teams. You can't turn on the pump without both the plumber and the mechanic.

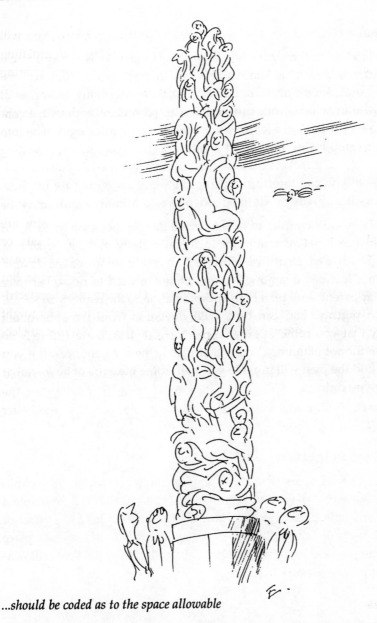

...should be coded as to the space allowable

The instrumentation engineer cannot carry out the cockpit maintenance without the electrician. These are examples of where several resources must be allocated together for the duration of the activity. Again, this needs to be coded into the affected activities.

Continuity

The standard and easy method of placing an activity is to require that it continues once it has started. This usually implies a continuous level of resource allocation throughout. But there are many examples of activities in which work can be interrupted and recontinued, ie the resources drop to zero for a while. You can't stop pouring cement, but you can stop laying bricks and painting walls. You can't stop putting up the piping brackets because the plumber is breathing down your neck, but you can interrupt lagging the pipes once they are in place. Again, each activity needs to be coded as to continuity requirements.

The above are examples of how intricate the planner's job really is. At first glance a network appears to be an orderly and rather simple, though crowded, structure. However, as you begin to see the detail it becomes less obvious how to plan, while the need to do so becomes more apparent. Any plan is an approximation to the reality you would like to portray, and can be a wild deviation from the subsequent reality that you come to experience. Nevertheless, inexactitude is no excuse for not planning. You will always achieve a better result if you plan, and the plan will provide you with some measure of how well or badly you did.

Chapter 9

Completing the Plan

Iucundi Acte Labores
(Completed Labours are Pleasant)

Cicero, 1st. Century B.C.

You will inevitably iterate the plan, possibly many times, before obtaining an initial live version that everyone concerned will agree to. The plan will be the best compromise you can make between managerial capacity, availability of resources, customer requirements, profitability and what you allow yourself to remember of disasters past. This chapter considers the managerial and contractual consequences of the plan that must be agreed to before it can be considered complete. This is where I think the general manager should come back into the game. The computer man needs to know how to actuate the management decisions, but the computer system must allow for management to be in charge.

Each activity needs an activity manager, someone responsible for getting the work done, and each manager will probably be responsible for a number of activities; perhaps a complete unit of the WBS. Obtaining the signatures of the activity managers is the best hope you have of success. All the signatures in the world are no guarantee of success, of course, but without them you have no come-back when the going gets tough.

Essentially you obtained commitment already at the initial planning meetings, but *Homo sapiens* is renowned for his bouts of amnesia, and you really need confirmation that when their several contributions were combined into a single entity it still made sense and was still realisable.

To make this easy your computer system should be able to group the activities by responsibility code. If each activity manager receives the complete plan not only can he see clearly what is expected of him, but also what the others are supposed to do. And the fact that the several components come from a single source prevents contradiction. Each knows that the others are meshed in logically.

A signature means that the activity manager understands what is to be done, that he won't be on vacation or otherwise engaged when the time comes, that he in turn has the guarantee of the people to do the work, as well as the equipment, materials and premises. It's a very tall order, and in practice very few project managers have the luxury of guarantees of anything before embarking on their projects. But computer technology at least makes it easy to see what is needed - what it is they *aren't* signing, if they aren't.

Having then published the plan for all to see, the initial version should be frozen in the computer. We call this the *baseline*. The baseline is the immutable target with which all subsequent progress is compared, and we shall see in Chapter 13 how this comparison is reported.

As work is done, and money expended, the value of the work done will hopefully increase, so the plan must provide the basis for the contractor to bill the client. It must contain some sort of formula for calculating the *earned value*, in contrast to accumulated cost. There must be no cause for debate after the starter's gun. How is this done?

The best basis, of course, for the contractor billing the client is completed work only, item by item. Earned value would then be zero until completion and would then jump to the agreed price for that item. But far too often, especially in long-term projects, it is found to be impossible to complete one item before other items are at or near completion, with the consequence that the contractor suffers an undue delay in payment. To allow the contractor to survive until final completion and handover we need something a little softer, something based on very rigorous planning.

A large project, one lasting over, say, two years will inevitably experience a progressive deterioration from the baseline, and the time comes when the accumulation of minor disasters becomes major enough to render the baseline useless for continued management purposes. The plan shall be born again; *revision one* of the baseline. Perhaps the first of a series of six-monthly revisions. Revisions are perfectly respectable, and are standard practice, but each one should be the result of some high-level pontification. They shouldn't just happen. They provide management of both customer and supplier with an opportunity of appraising the situation, in particular of reviewing the contract. The problem in the bad old days was that management at the rarefied levels found it very difficult to determine why things were the way they were, and such meetings were often therefore not uncharged with emotion. But a good computer system can change all that, substituting information for opinion.

And here we come to the Chinese mirrors bit. At the activity level management has an excellent understanding of what is going on. Each activity will have a well-defined start. Its progress will be paved with drawings, all systematically numbered, or tangible measurable objects. The costs will be accurately collected, and when the activity is finished the computer will be told so. Getting it all right is the tangible stuff of line management. But as you start combining activities into larger and larger units in the WBS it becomes progressively more difficult to measure and therefore to understand. If some activities are finished ahead of time, some on time and some behind time are you ahead of the game or not? What does it mean to add, in some way, the progress being made on disparate parts of a whole? If the cost to date is below schedule is it because of your brilliant fiscal control, or is it because you can get neither the stuff nor the staff? Clearly you need a strategic picture of the cost tied in with a strategic picture of what you have done with the money. Hence a way of depicting macroscopic progress in the light of a macroscopic version of the baseline. What does a macroscopic version of the baseline look like? The problem is that of having to add the incommensurable. You can't add wiring and plumbing, or wood and concrete. You can only add numbers derived from these actions and materials.

But what numbers? Their weight? Their cost per kilo? The number of days to go to completion? The number of man-days of effort? The price of undelivered parts? And so on. Somehow it all has to be reduced to a common denominator, and this is bound to be fairly arbitrary and subject to judgement. The trick is to exercise the judgement at as low a level as possible, and clothe the judgement in a formula; make it look at the higher levels as though it isn't judgement. Above all, don't give the lawyers any scope for exercising their judgement.

The traditional yardstick, for want of something better, is the notion of *percent complete*. (If you find something better, let us know.) Once this is defined you have the basis for earned value. The basic idea is this. If you estimated ten man-days to do a job, and you have used five, provided your estimate was correct the job is 50% complete. By somehow aggregating the percent complete of the disparate activities you could compute the percent complete of the whole. But immediately you are overwhelmed by a welter of objections. Suppose your original estimates were wrong. You might well not know this at the 50% point. But by the original 80% point you might have found that you were really only 40% complete, and the original estimate had to be doubled.

To press home the problem of percent complete, is your house 100% complete? What is it then? And what does your spouse say?

Even supposing you can measure accurately the progress of an individual activity, how can you combine several? How can you add 50% of one activity to 40% of another? Is the result 45%? Or should you somehow weight them proportionately to their individual cost? Fifty percent of a $10,000 activity plus 40% of a $20,000 might come to a combined 43% complete. But what does it mean physically? Does it really tell you anything?

Anyway, how do you measure? Are money spent or man-hours consumed indicative? Is value proportional to cost? How about drawings? If you are expecting twenty drawings does ten mean 50%? Only if they are similar in size and difficulty. How about components in a WBS substructure? How do you add cranks and camshafts? Bolts and batteries?

What is the purpose of the upper levels of the WBS? Why do we perform these numerical gymnastics? Can we not leave reviews at the network level where progress means something?

The question is of course rhetorical. It would mean the upper levels of management abdicating all responsibility. But there is something more to it than that. Payment. That and the reconciliation of two fundamentally opposed interests. The supplier would like to be paid the full amount on signing the contract. The customer, on the other hand, would prefer to pay nothing until the whole thing has been delivered and been shown to work properly. This could put the supplier out of business, so a compromise has to be struck - progress payments. Hence progress measurement, arbitrary though it may be. Hence percent complete. But remember, percent complete means what you

...is your house 100% complete?

define it to mean; what for contractual purposes you and your customer agree it shall mean.

The main objection to the use of percent complete is that it is usually based on the initial estimates of durations, making no allowance for changes based on the ensuing reality. But durations have a habit of increasing as the project progresses, and with them the number of manhours expended. If the actual number of man-hours reaches and exceeds the original estimate there is an obvious danger that the percent complete may exceed 100. To obviate that you can proceed as follows. At the freezing of the network the baseline is aggregated up the WBS as labour and non-labour cost per component. See Figure 9.1.

During the life of the project, costs are aggregated up the WBS to be compared with the baseline costs. The percent complete of an individual activity can be defined as the number of man-hours expended to date divided by the *current estimate* of the total man-hours required; ie if the latter is increased the percent complete will actually decrease, giving the impression of negative work. In this way, however, percent complete will never exceed 100.

The percent complete of each WBS component at the bottom level can then be the total number of man-hours expended to date on the activities leading to that component, divided by the total current estimates for those activities. And for billing purposes the earned value can be defined as a predetermined fraction of the percent complete multipled by the agreed completed value of the component.

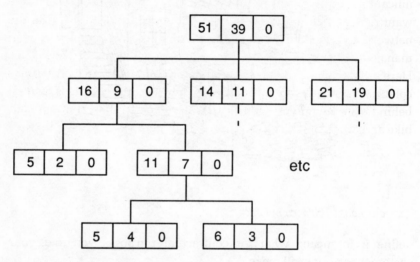

Figure 9.1 Each WBS component consists of three elements, estimated labour cost on the left, estimated material cost in the middle and percent complete on the right (initial value zero)

The same definition can be extended, level by level, to the top, remembering that at any review point the percent complete can actually decrease, despite an increase in the work done. You are always working with the latest estimates of duration and effort. After all, these are much more accurate than those of the original plan. One thing you certainly gain as you make progress is understanding of what it's all about. You may not be finished yet, but by golly you've learnt a lot. Plough that sobering experience back into the management numbers, and be honest about it.

The frozen components of the WBS become the *management milestones* of the project; major chunks of official progress that are fully paid for upon completion, but that can be partially paid for before completion, provided for in the contract. The contract must of course allow for decreases in percent complete. But these will also be part of baseline revisions as overruns are absorbed.

As a footnote to the discussion of the project baseline, my personal feeling is that senior managers confine themselves far too readily to high-level statistical management. Statistics often blurs the vision. The broad view all to easily blinds you to individual elements that can sabotage the whole caboodle. A potential saboteur can be a very insignificant item in the total picture if you judge it solely on cost. For the want of a nail an empire was lost. The nails are deep down in the network, so when the mumbo-jumbo about percents complete is over, management should be asking questions down at the network level. Here's where you find the undiluted information. And if it's critical it's coloured red. The ultimate question is, which single activity is furthest behind? The computer will tell you, and you can then jump on your bike and be a real manager for once.

The computer makes it easy for you

Chapter 10

A Project Database

It is a Capital Mistake to Theorise Before one has Data

Sherlock Holmes

The core of a plan is the network, a numerical device containing logic and time at the very minimum, and also the possibility of containing information about the resources required to do the work. If you wish you can leave it at that. But as the project manager gains experience, and his level of expectation rises, he has the possibility of adding extra functions to the core, thereby increasing the value of his planning system. And the computer man needs to know how to do this.

The basic element of the plan is the individual activity, and we are able to *link* that activity to any other information that takes our fancy; anything that can be related in some way to that activity. The only proviso to what is described in this chapter is that you use an *open* system, as discussed in Chapters 14 and 15.

In this chapter we shall simply list some of these extra functions as examples. No doubt you will produce your own as you gain experience. While the computer details lie outside the scope of this book, the important point to be made is that you can be master of your own destiny here and can quite easily specify additional functions for incorporation into the system as they occur to you.

Probably the easiest one to begin with is Personnel. If you use the system to schedule people you can automatically calculate the cost of the labour by linking the Personnel database, which contains the labour rates, with the network, which contains the hours.

The other main resource is materials. Since these have to be ordered, an obvious candidate is the Purchase Order database. To obtain the budgeted cost of materials link the network to the Materials Prices database. In turn, as materials are issued to the project, the aggregated chronological requirements form the basis for monitoring their flow. The total agglomeration becomes the Procurement function, and the person responsible can seek comfort in the fact that his instructions emanate automatically from the details of the work, and armed with a little statistics and an appropriate computer program he might be able to close down his warehouse and save the company some money. That alone could pay for the planning system a thousand times over.

As work is performed and progress made, the details can be entered into the system. An obvious candidate here is the Timesheet system. If all work is registered against its activity number, the actual hours expended can be linked to the network for comparison with the estimates and for computing the actual costs. Indeed, the simplest conceivable work sheet is one consisting of the planned activities. All you need to report are the variances from the plan. The very roots of exception reporting! One not to be despised reward for sticking to the plan is no timesheet to fill in on a Friday.

The work involved in each activity may either generate engineering drawings or require them to be issued from the drawing office. Either way, the activity number can be linked to the Drawing Register such that each drawing contains reference to the pertaining activity. This leads to foolproof identification.

The same holds for the other documents pertaining to an activity; parts lists, assembly instructions, maintenence procedures, training manuals etc. How often in your company do these things get forgotten, confused or misnumbered? By linking the Document Register to the network you can automatically remind people of what is needed and get the results properly identified.

In addition to the practical activities of the plan, management has the opportunity of superimposing (or infiltrating) pseudo activities concerned with company policy, standards etc. that have to be complied with to complete the job. In particular, in this day and age of international agreements, standards definers such as ISO 9000 could well be incorporated automatically. A Standards database would give management the comfortable assurance that their decrees were being adhered to in the heat of battle.

At a higher level the Project Milestones may be regarded as a little database in their own right, especially if you are running several projects in parallel. If the Milestone Register is linked to all the networks, top management has an automatic monitoring device for all its income-generating work.

Indeed, it begins to look as though the planning network can be made to be the core of everything you do in your company. This thought brings one on to think about the differences between the projects, our starting point in this book, and corporate headquarters. Some of the databases mentioned here are obviously peculiar to the project. They are created when the project starts and die (hopefully not of old age) when it finishes. Others, however, are company databases and live for ever.

The fundamental difference between them is that corporate databases are something common to all company functions, be they projects or otherwise. Moreover the total corporate database is more stable in structure and relatively slow in growth, whereas a project database takes on a life, builds up from something quite small, and eventually disappears.

What comes out loud and clear here is that there is a lot of data flow between corporate databases and project databases, and it is therefore vital that the computer technology used by the company permits this data flow in an effortless way to the users. Having said that, in most companies today, despite (or perhaps because of) four decades of computer development, the corporate and project data systems are two almost water-tight quantities. Very few companies have yet established a fluent corporate-project information system, so here's a challenge for you.

To complete the picture there is an additional function that won't come of its own accord, but that can have enormous value if we create it. A corporate experience database.

Each project is a new experience. At the outset most projects are brave new adventures, while at its close every project is a sobering story of real-life vicissitudes. We mount new projects in the same eternal spirit of optimism that brought palaeolithic man blinking out of his cave, unconcerned that there were sabre-tooth tigers waiting behind the next rock. The only difference is that we've done it before. Time and time again. The same old tigers. The problem is we ignore the past and live in hope that the future by some miracle will be different to the past and be free of disasters. Hence our estimates are hopelessly short - even if we are clever enough to think of all the activities.

Far better to collect the experience gained in the past in some automatic way and feed it into the planning stage of the next project. If we can systematically accumulate experience and make planning as automatic as possible we will stand a much better chance of getting it right. So the idea is a corporate experience database. At the close of each project the database is updated and made available as the first step of the next project. (We shall return to this idea at the end of Chapter 15 when we discuss the question of using the planning system to increase the hit rate in sending out bids.)

The idea of an experience database presupposes that the company undertakes similar types of project. You must be able to accumulate experience of similar things. If it's a factory last time and a dam this time the past won't help too much, but if it's blocks of flats every time we stand a chance. So the last database could be a structured set of statistics that passes back from the project to the corporate database.

In summary, what this chapter has tried to do is alert you to the possibility of progressively adding data and functions to your planning system, as you gain experience and confidence, and to keep a look out for profitable examples, appropriate to your unique circumstances.

...brought paleolithic man blinking out of his cave

Chapter 11

Using the System - 1: Telling it What is Happening

> Nothing in progression can rest on its original plan. We may as well think of rocking a grown man in the cradle of an infant
>
> *Edmund Burke, 1780*

We have discussed now most of the components of a typical planning and control system. The next step is to discuss its use, and this chapter and the next take the project manager and his computer man through a fair bit of detail. This is by far the harder part, and it's where a lot of well-meant intentions become paving-stones. It is much easier to create a plan than to carry it out. It is easy enough these days to implement a set of procedures inside a computer. It is, sorry to say, getting less easy to persuade people to use them. The fundamental problem is that the computer, because it is a *procedure* machine, imposes procedures on those who use it, ie discipline. People who are in daily contact with computer systems become extensions to those systems, and they don't like it. We shall dwell upon this problem later in this chapter, but as you read it please bear in mind that in reality we are talking more about people than about machines. Indeed, there must be a Nobel Peace Prize for the person who solves the man-machine problem once and for all as far as computers are concerned.

A lot of people make networks to help them plan the project, remember all the things that need to be done, get them in the right order, and determine the probable life time of the project, together with its cost. But when the project starts they promptly discard the network, perhaps leaving it pinned up on the wall as monument to their managerial skills. Now there is, actually, a reasonable excuse for this. Traditionally it has been very cumbersome and time-consuming to keep a network alive once the project has started. Computer technology hadn't kept pace with the needs of the project manager. If you had no hope of making the network agree with reality in all respects it was better to leave it well alone. Nothing worse than a half-truth.

But with every project, the initial plan drifts slowly away from reality (sometimes quickly), so if you can you should report reality back to the plan, and change the plan accordingly. This implies that the network must contain the possibility of enabling this to happen; to have an updating function related to it via the activity number.

How often should you report progress? Obviously with a period that fits in naturally with the project. In most cases this is monthly, and the process of doing so is called the *cut-off*.

What information do you want to report back to the network at each cut-off? An obvious example is actual start. For some reason or other an activity may have been delayed in starting. If the actual start is later than the scheduled latest start, ie if all the total float has been used up, a reschedule will lead to a delay in project completion. A new critical path may emerge, and the project leader may have to have his eye on a new ball.

If an activity has an actual start it must also have an actual finish or a remaining duration. The latter may well exceed the original estimation of the duration, but at least it is based on recent experience and not on pure optimism.

Another example is time spent on an activity, possibly leading to the calculation of percent complete and earned value as described in Chapter 9. This problem manifests itself in earnest when all the original estimated time and money have been used up but the activity hasn't been finished. This calls for a re-estimate of the activity duration and budget, and yet another reschedule.

As each activity is completed the completion date should be input. This automatically triggers the start of succeeding activities.

Cost data should also be reported back to the network, labour costs, machinery costs, the costs of materials issued, and indeed anything the project leader needs to manage the project.

Updating a plan is not something to be taken on lightly. You must either do it rigorously or not at all. If you do it half-heartedly you can easily fool yourself that you know what's going on. The trouble with reports is that they all look equally convincing.

If you are going to keep the plan alive you will need cast-iron discipline and some well-trained, dedicated people backed up with clear procedures and good documentation. As we have said, the people who work directly with a computer system are part of that system. This is an insidious truth of the late twentieth century. But if we are going to have modern people working with modern computers, as a total, reliable system, we have to make it easy. And, if we can, we ought to make it fun.

The first thing of importance is to make the terminal or PC screen easy to understand and use. It must be easy to see what data goes where, how to get it there and how to ensure that it is right. By clever use of messages from the computer it should be easy to coach the user in what he has to know, and to provide help in times of panic. Generally speaking we have reached a point in computer technology today where screen forms, as they are called, have become harmonised with the people using them. (This is only a very recent development. In the early days of computing there were almost insurmountable barriers interposed between computer and user, and the user had to bend to the computer.)

To help the user find his way in a system we usually make use of a hierarchy of menus. A menu is a list (preferably short) of options that the user may select at each point in the system. Usually the choice is between entering yet one more record of data or of leaving this menu for the next. Or it may be the choice of interrogating data, changing it, deleting it or obtaining a report now that the data is (hopefully) correct.

The evolution of screen management on the PC or computer terminal is in a very rapid phase at the time of writing. New techniques are being invented almost daily in the quest for that Nobel Prize. It isn't the details of any particular system that are important here, but the basic principles involved.

Imagine now that young lady with the white coat clutching a mighty arm full of tatty pink sheets, the project progress forms, filled in the previous week on the site. She sits down at the computer terminal to the following picture:

```
MENU OF CURRENT PROJECTS

1        CENTRAL HOSPITAL
2        STATION EXTENSION
3        CHEESE FACTORY
4        TOGETHERNESS APARTMENTS
5        FRED'S FABULOUS FUNLAND
6        DRISNOW SKISLOPE

10       EXIT

KEY IN CHOICE AND PRESS "ENTER" .....>
```

She selects an appropriate project, 4 say, and obtains the next menu:

```
TOGETHERNESS APARTMENTS

MAIN MENU

1        MONTHLY PROGRESS UPDATE
2        MATERIALS RECEIVED
3        MATERIALS ISSUED
4        CALCULATIONS
5        STANDARD REPORTS - PRINTED
6        STANDARD REPORTS - PLOTTED
7        CHANGES TO PLAN

10       RETURN TO PROJECT MENU

KEY IN CHOICE AND PRESS "ENTER" .....>
```

This menu tells her that there are seven distinct things she can do with the Togetherness Apartments system, and that when she has finished she is invited to return control to the project menu so that she or someone else can use the terminal for one of the other projects. Suppose she enters a 1. This produces the following menu:

```
TOGETHERNESS APARTMENTS

MONTHLY PROGRESS UPDATE MENU

1        HOURS BY ACTIVITY
2        NON-LABOUR COSTS BY ACTIVITY
3        PERCENT COMPLETE BY ACTIVITY
4        ACTUAL STARTS AND FINISHES

10       RETURN TO MAIN MENU

KEY IN CHOICE AND PRESS "ENTER" .....>
```

Again, a small number of options, including returning to the main menu. Suppose, again, she enters a 1. Now she comes to the rock-bottom level; the level where data can actually be entered. To do this the lady needs an electronic form.

This menu tells her...

And now for a little history. If the eighteenth century was the Age of Enlightenment, and the nineteeth the Industrial Revolution, the twentieth century will probably go down in history as the Age of the Form. With the exponential rise of legislation and industry since about 1914, society has become hell-bent on formalising the collection of information. This process received a sharp acceleration with the advent of the computer, and there must be a distinct danger that the jungles of the Amazon will soon disappear to provide the necessary paper.

The end of the form, as we know it, is not yet in sight, and the only comfort that we can offer is that if you use an electronic version of a form, as opposed to paper, there is a better than even chance that you will get it right. You won't miss out any of the vital fields, and your grosser mistakes will be spotted.

What might the Worked Hours by Activity form look like?

Figure 11.1 is a typical simplified example.

When the form appears on the screen the first field, PERSON NO. is highlighted. When a number has been entered the next field is highlighted, ACTIVITY NO., and so on until all four fields have been entered. At this point the young lady may pause to check that she has entered the data correctly. When satisfied that she has she presses the

```
                    TOGETHERNESS APARTMENTS

              WORKED HOURS BY ACTIVITY : WEEK NO. 17

      PERSON NO.        .......      ACTIVITY NO. .......
      NORMAL HOURS      .......      O'TIME HOURS .......


      TO ENTER THE FULL PAGE PRESS THE F6 KEY
      TO RETURN TO THE MENU PRESS THE F10 KEY
```

Figure 11.1 Typical electronic version of a form

F6 key to transfer the complete record to the relevant data table, automatically clearing the field positions. Normally she would follow this with another record, but eventually she will have completed the task and will press the F10 key, say, to return control to the Monthly Progress Update menu.

As was intimated a moment ago, one of the great advantages of using electronic forms is that it can help you do the job properly. What this means is that you can build into the computer automatic checks and a modicum of guidance. Firstly, the highlighted field forces the user to enter the data in the right place. The person number will have a certain format, and if this format is not adhered to the field can be made to blink, say, forcing the user to correct the error. Of course, we cannot guarantee that the person number is entirely correct. Two digits may be interposed, for example, producing a legal number, though a wrong one. The same for the activity number. The next test might be for repetition. If the same person works on a particular activity twice within a week, this might be an error.

Again, both fields flashing, forcing the operator to take action to get the data accepted. Normal hours will have a limit, probably 40. Overtime can only be entered if normal hours have reached a certain minimum, say 35, and itself will probably have an upper limit, say 20.

We call this process of built-in checks, validation. We shall discuss this in a little more detail in a moment.

A menu item of particular importance is no. 7 in the main menu, CHANGES TO PLAN. Remember that the system will contain the baseline, the first version of the plan, frozen in ice, and any change to the plan can be depicted in relation to the baseline. If the project continues for much more than a year the baseline itself can be brought up to date, every six months, say, and a succession of versions retained for comparison purposes.

This gives you a fair idea of how a user finds his way to the heart of the system, enters records of data, and finds his way back again to the periphery. A good system makes this very easy. None of your $ signs or asterisks! It also helps you minimise the scope for error, although it cannot eliminate it entirely.

It is easy, but it is terribly boring. Feeding a computer with data as a full-time job must be one of the most soul-destroying activities on the face of this earth. The people who do it are the daughters of the key-punch girls of old, and one wonders what their children are going to be doing. This isn't a book about sociology, nevertheless realise that boredom leads to error, and your system is as good as the truthfulness of the data it contains.

It is therefore perhaps of interest to dwell a little more on the business of validation before going over to a discussion of avoiding the problem altogether. The problem is paper.

... boredom leads to error

Before you can bring data to the computer it has to be generated and much of it written on bits of paper. This is an ancient problem that we'll always have. And there are two aspects to it, the design of the form they come on, and the legibility of people's writing. The former shouldn't be a problem. It should only be a question of having the same person design the screen form and the paper form. But even then you have the problem that while you can program a computer to scream at you if you input the wrong data, it is very difficult to do the same with paper. It doesn't matter how much you try to tell some people, they will write things on paper that simply don't obey the rules, the number of characters in a part number, the sequence day-month-year in date field, the proper spelling of the units involved.

Illegibility is an incurable disease, and there are some people who simply mustn't be issued pencil and paper.

But what's this about rules? Aren't we free to use the computer how we like? No, we aren't, sorry to say. Not once the system is written. When a programmer starts to think about a new system it's all in the mind, and he can think what he likes; unbounded imagination. But as he starts to design and implement he starts to make *rules* for the computer, and when he has finished he has created a whole onion-shaped conglomeration of rules that *must* be followed if the system is to work properly. Furthermore, the people who work in direct contact with the system must obey rules just as stringent as those inside the computer, so there's at least one layer of the onion outside the machine itself.

To help enforce the rules, and do the screaming, a system should contain validation tests. Examples of these are:

- A numerical field is only allowed to contain numbers. It may also have maximum and minimum limits.
- An alphabetical field will have a maximum number of characters, eg eight.
- A date field will have a fixed format, eg DD-MM-YYYY.

A validation test will make it impossible for you to break the rules, but there are limits to what it can do. It would prevent you keying in 12-13-1995 for 13-12-1995, but it wouldn't prevent you keying in 11-12-1995 for 12-11-1995.

Beyond that the rules may not be quite so stringent, but they are there. And as time goes on, and the computer becomes more and more central to the business of running the project and running the business, the onion will grow to envelop much of the organisation.

The next set of rules beyond inputting the data correctly are those about when the data needs to arrive at the terminal. Whether this is to be done on a regular basis, or at random. Where? Centrally at one place, or decentrally out in the departments. Then rules about producing results. How? Printed or plotted? When and where, and to whom?

There's nothing new here really. It's just company procedures, and the only difference is that they have to be obeyed much more strictly than in the old days. The computer, though a slave, is much more demanding than any boss.

But the rewards are worth it! Discipline buys you control, control buys you profit, and that Nobel Prize will bring you fame (and some fortune).

But not all updating needs to be manual. Because of the problems we have just discussed we should aim to minimise human intervention as much as possible and try to make all input automatic; to arrange for data to be trapped automatically at source and transferred automatically to the computer, and then automatically into data tables.

Hand-in-hand with the development of the computer there has been an equivalent development of data acquisition and communications. This development has taken place since the early 1960s, and today a great deal of the information generated by equipment and people in the working world is accessed automatically. This is particularly true in factory environments where processes lend themselves well to instrumentation, and badge readers make it easy to follow the progress of parts in production, and the time spent by the trades and disciplines on each task. The technology is there. It is up to each organisation and project to replace pencil-form-terminal with instrument-digitiser-communications line.

Today the place to start is with the engineering drawing. Computer-aided design has now emerged from the experimental and pioneering phase, and has become an accepted technology. A CAD system contains enormous amounts of information fundamental to the project; the drawings themselves, the drawing numbers, accompanying text, materials information, parts information, etc. All of this is potential input to a project control system, and it is up to the project leader to decide what he needs rather than it being a technological problem of what he can get.

The remaining links in the chain depend on the details of the project. They may be the automatic registration of parts and materials received; the automatic acknowledgment of successful quality control;

the automatic message that one process has completed and the next started; that the part in process has reached a new factory position; that Joe Bloggs has arrived at work and is now engaged on a particular job in a particular area.

What you decide to do is a question of economics. No one is asking you to be a pioneer any more. There are far more opportunities for data automation than you could usefully employ. They work and they are reliable.

And that is the key. Reliability. However friendly you make the ordinary terminal, however good the documentation, however well trained the people, you will always have problems. People simply are not machines, and we ought to be using machines to make people's lives more human, and not less. The result will always be increased profitability.

At the receiving end, automatic data is stored in computer files available to whatever systems need them, and in most cases it is a straight-forward programmatic task to convert the data from its raw format to the format of data tables as we have discussed them.

The technology is there. Use it and get the people out of the loop.

Chapter 12

Using the System - 2: Reporting Progress to the Users

This Blessed Plot

Shakespeare, Richard II

The whole point of collecting and manipulating data is to ready it for action of one sort and another. It isn't there for academic reasons. Action falls broadly into one of two categories, either it is direct in the form of a transaction, or indirect in the form of a report; either it is something in its own right, or *informs* about something so that someone (or something) else can perform an evaluation and take some further form of action. To the extent that criteria can be embedded in a computer program, decisions can be delegated to the computer in the safe knowledge that it will always do the right thing. When they cannot, then the people around it have to apply criteria of their own. However, as the development of computers has rendered it possible, more and more decisions have been delegated to the computer. It's safer that way.

Examples of direct action output are tickets (airline, theatre etc), orders for materials and equipment, bills for work done or deliveries made, cheques for payment, and reminders to pay your Reader's Digest subscription, even though you've already paid it.

The other kind of output, call it passive output, is essentially reports to people of what has happened.

The key to success here is to make it trivially easy to produce reports the way the users would like to have them, and not the way some computer programmer happens to have designed them. And it must be easy to change them, to add to the information they contain, to delete unwanted information, to summarise large amounts of data into digestible quantities, and to present reality as a comparison with expectations.

You've got yourself a plan consisting of a WBS and a network surrounded by a galaxy of data tables, some exquisite documentation, a well-trained staff of dedicated people, a web of data-acquisition equipment and a live project. What are you going to do with it? What do you want it to do for you? What do you want it to tell you? How? How often? What do you want it to tell other people? Your staff? The store-keeper? The accounts department ? The document control group? The customer? The subcontractors? The auditors? How much do they need to know? How little do they really need to know?

Fundamentally, whatever information you report back to those departments, it must always be done with reference to the baseline, bought off by management and the customer, and used as the ultimate control mechanism for the project. The baseline is produced from the WBS and the network, each playing its appropriate role. The WBS is the easier one to forecast from the cost point of view. The drawing system produces the lists of materials and components, each of which has a price obtainable from the rate book.

Estimating the work required to join all the components together is the trick. This is where experience comes in, and still today this experience is mostly in human form. Estimates are based on memory, curried with large dollops of optimism.

Periodical updating (weekly, monthly) can be done via either the WBS or the network, or a combination, depending on the system you use. If you only have a network you can report both time and materials against activity numbers, and aggregate up an *implicit* WBS to the required levels. If you only have a WBS (you have somehow made your schedule without the use of a network) you can report time and materials against WBS elements and aggregate up an *explicit* WBS. If you have both, you can report work against activities and materials against the WBS.

If you want to monitor the work and manage the project you need a network. A WBS doesn't contain time as an entity, and therefore you cannot report remaining work, expected completion date and therefore expected next start. Monitoring costs alone, however, can be done with a WBS. By some sort of magic you estimate expenditure over the life of the project, create a baseline and report periodically at the WBS working level, comparing actuals with baseline. However, if actuals exceed budget you can find out where, but not usually why.

If materials cost more than expected, this will show on a WBS, but if work costs more it is difficult to find out why because there is no basis for work comparisons.

This is not a book about detailed cost accounting or value engineering, and I do not propose therefore to dwell upon these things in any depth. However, because it is about how we use the computer to deal with the large number of numbers generated in a project, we should make particular mention of the problem of measuring the value of the work carried out at any point in time.

In any large project, at any point in time, there will be a large amount of partially finished work. The question is, how much is this partially finished work worth? How much ought the subcontractors to be able to bill? Well, at one extreme it could be argued that incomplete work has no value. There is no absolute guarantee that it will ever finish. The whole consists of the sum of its parts, and nothing works until it all works.

However, it is not the intention of the project to put its subcontractors out of business. The cash of the subcontractors must be kept flowing to keep them alive until the final bill may be submitted.

In Chapter 9 we introduced the idea of earned value, the basis of a compromise agreed to and enshrined in the contract. The project accepts a percentage of the effort expended as a measure of its value. This is made manifest in the chain of milestones, a series of major progress achievement points; the completion of certain key activities. It is used by company management as a strategic control mechanism over project management, and as a series of major billing points.

The goal of the subcontractor is to make the value of the work exceed the cost of doing it. However, if he fails to achieve this he will do what he can to obtain an adjustment to the contract. All such changes should be reported as soon as possible to the system, and made the subject of Variation Orders (VOs), a euphemism for holding out your cap. However, often the fault lies with the customer, who has changed his design and requires a rework. Often the management of VOs becomes a major factor in a project management system.

These paragraphs give you some idea of the uses a system can be put to. Once the system is in place there is no end to these and no end to the different views people will have of it. Consequently, a good reporting facility is vital to the intelligent and profitable use of the system. That is what the remainder of this chapter is about.

...there will be a large amount of partially finished work

There are basically two ways of reporting, either printing columns of numbers or drawing pictures. The traditional method is the former, and in many ways it is one of the worst things we have done in the whole history of computing. At first printing wasn't a problem. It hardly existed. It was so slow that you had to think very carefully before you printed anything. But by about 1960 we started to get printers that printed a thousand lines a minute, and you could do it without slowing the computer down. So wheelbarrows and fork-lift trucks were brought into play, forests were mown down, and the number you were looking for was there somewhere, deeply hidden in a huge heap of paper. This gave computing a very bad name, coupled with the fact that the output was so terribly cryptic. The high-speed printer stopped programmers having to think, and the inflexibility of formatting reports made it difficult anyway to respond to the genuine needs of the user.

All this has now changed, however, and today's ease of creating and modifying report formats has led to decent legibility and effortless development. There is no excuse today for a programmer producing thick reports or unintelligible ones.

Moreover, if you think of the computer as an electronic book, what is displayed on the screen is also a printed page. This means that you can play around with a report format electronically until you are happy with it, and then press the print button.

But however clear your print format you cannot escape the fact that numbers are very difficult to digest mentally if there are more than seven of them. The project manager's job is controlling his project via the numbers it produces. We said that right at the start. A project is a giant number generator, and the manager a vulnerable, would-be number-absorber. What can we do to stop his getting numerical indigestion?

The answer to this, of course, is pictures. A single line consists of an infinite number of points, each one of which may represent a number. So, in principle a single drawn line is worth a thousand pages of printed numbers. Well, if that's a slight exaggeration, it's nevertheless true to say that a well-designed single page of lines can represent a thick wad of printed numbers, and do it in a way that the latter cannot hope to achieve. The human brain is quite incapable of extracting trends from lists, of comparing behaviours, of spotting the essential. Our numerical systems were invented for the purpose of calculation, not for the presentation of results.

Computer graphics was also born about 1960, and has evolved to a point of sophistication today that has made it cheap, accessible and very individual. There are now very powerful graphical report generators that allow you to represent masses of data in a wide variety of ways. To each according to his need.

But this is only talk. Better to see examples. They speak for themselves.

To the project manager the most important picture to start with is his network. Although the network is represented in the computer numerically, and can be displayed as such on the screen, there is no way you can visualise it numerically. True, each basic number is input by the user, but one at a time. He doesn't input the whole array of numbers as an entity. The entity can only be beheld when it has been drawn. A network is an array of lines, not a bunch of numbers.

A well-drawn network is a very powerful tool. The constraints need to be easy to follow, the activities legibly displayed, and the critical path must punch you between the eyes. Colour it red. Depict clearly which activities have been finished, which are active, perhaps percent complete, and which have not yet started - especially those that should have. To do the job properly it is best to use a plotter that takes a roll of paper rather than a page. Some networks are long!

From the network the most obvious derived picture is the bar chart or gantt chart, the activities time-scaled, sorted in some useful order, appropriately coloured and annotated. It is the bar chart that is probably the most useful management tool for tracking progress, and a well-designed one will depict at a glance the actual situation compared with the plan. A further refinement of the bar chart is the linked or logic bar chart which shows the dependence of the activities on one another, as in the network.

Because the bar chart is so important we should spend a little time discussing how to use it properly. On day 1 the activities may all be plotted as empty bars indicating initial estimates of duration, placed in the order of early start, say. The non-critical ones may also have their floats indicated by, say, dotted lines, as shown in Figure 12.1.

From Figure 12.1 can you construct the network? Which is the critical path? Is it a coincidence that Activities 2 and 4 have the same total float?

After the project has started, and worked hours have been reported against the activities, the question arises as to how best to display progress. It is all too easy to fool yourself. On the other hand it is all too easy to cover the plot in polychromatic explanation, resulting in total confusion. So be careful.

The easiest thing to do is simply plot the bar chart with the report date (time now) as a vertical line, and with everything to the left shaded as though it were completed work; see Figure 12.2.

Such a plot is worse than useless since it gives the reader the impression that everything is on schedule.

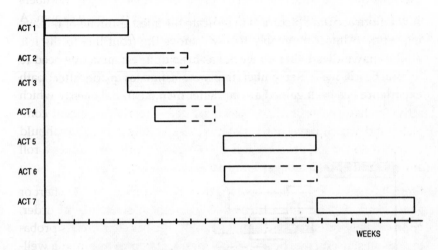

Figure 12.1 Example of a bar chart
All activities shown starting at early start. Total float dotted

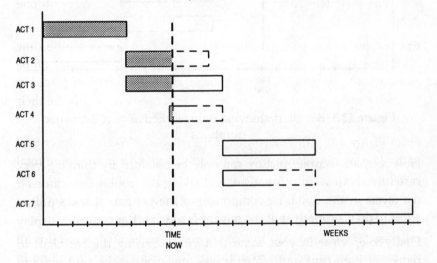

Figure 12.2 Bar chart showing time now

Slightly less misinformative is to display man-hours worked as a percentage of the estimated durations. See Figure 12.3 (page 94).

The thick line is called the FRONT LINE, and the picture gives an instant impression of the extent to which the project is on schedule.

But the problem here is that the shaded areas do not necessarily indicate work remaining to be done. An accurate picture needs a little more work.

A yet more accurate picture is to indicate the latest estimate of remaining work. Almost inevitably this will move the front line to the left. And it may indicate that no work has been done on an activity, when in practice it has. Remember that new estimates made after some experience has been gained are far better than the initial ones.

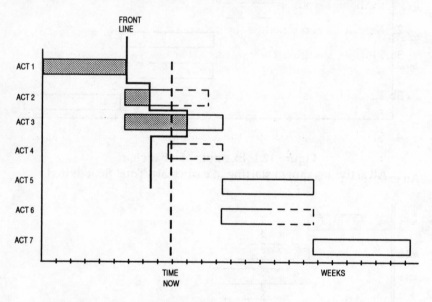

Figure 12.3 Bar chart showing time worked as % of estimated durations

However, an accurate picture can only be obtained by thinking very carefully about what is involved, and taking the trouble to include all the facets in the updating component of the system. It takes a little effort to do it properly, but the reward is much better control.

Firstly keep clear in your mind that you are using the bar chart to represent both time and effort; weeks and man-weeks. But you are doing so without any explicit indication of the number of resources. It's a bit of a Chinese mirror trick, and you can easily fool yourself. Stated simply, the duration of an activity is the total work divided by the resources applied to it. And both can vary. You can revise your estimate of remaining work as you gain experience, and the actual resources may fluctuate, while your original estimate was probably constant. Moreover, some of the work done might have been completely wasted.

There should be nothing sacred about the initial estimates. We should revise them at every opportunity as reality replaces theory.

So what do we do? A comprehensive procedure at each reporting point consists of the following:

1. Estimate remaining durations based on remaining work and available resources.

2. Reanalyse and schedule the network.

3a. Plot the resulting activities as a bar chart showing original start and current finish estimates.

3b. Replot the previous version alongside as a basis for comparison.

4. Shade each bar to show the amount of work completed as a proportion of the total new duration.

An example of a single activity is seen in Figure 12.4.

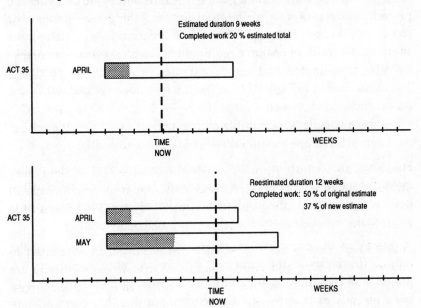

Figure 12.4 Comparative bar charts with re-estimates of duration

Be warned that not everyone takes this much trouble, but anything less can easily fool you, and your boss will want to know why the project has been 99% complete for half its life, with the end still not in sight.

As well as comparing this month's progress with last, for example, you would want a similar plot comparing this month's with the baseline.

A particularly useful version of bar chart is the *Responsibility Bar chart*. If each activity contains the initials of the person responsible for carrying it out, a bar chart can be grouped by initials making it easy for each manager to see his own responsibilities at a glance, and for each to see the others'. This is particularly useful if the participants are scattered far and wide early in the planning stage. It is an excellent document for obtaining people's commitment or discovering early on that something won't work. Signing and returning the responsibility bar chart makes it a contract between project manager and activity managers.

The next control picture is that of resource availability and requirement. This is normally portrayed via a *histogram*, one per resource type, over the period of the project. The importance of the resource histogram is that it shows at a glance which resources are delaying the project, and serves as a visible tool for smoothing requirements or chasing deliveries. Figures 12.5 and 12.6 are examples of histograms showing the result of resource requirement (welders) versus availability after time-limited and resource-limited scheduling respectively. The shaded areas in Figure 12.5 show the resource overload, while the areas enclosed between dotted lines in both show underload - resources available but unusable on this project. Note that the project has been delayed one month because of resource unavailability.

Following the depiction of the material project is that of the consequent budget and costs. There is a cosmic law which states that the latter always exceeds the former, and the job of the project manager is to minimise the discrepancy.

A picture of the cumulative budget with time has the shape of the letter S (in theory at any rate) and is therefore called an S-curve. A project had two limiting S-curves, one supposing that every activity starts as early as possible and the other supposing that every activity starts as late as possible. Then, if the estimates are good, any actual S-curve will lie somewhere between the two. If the S-curve of actual expenditure lies to the left of the area the project is in trouble, if it lies to the right someone isn't reporting something.

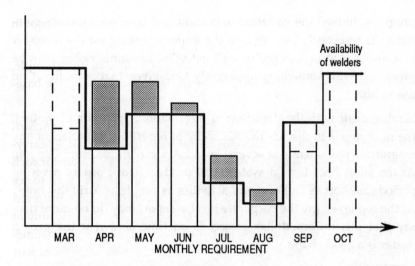

Figure 12.5 Histogram showing requirement vs availability after time-limited schedule

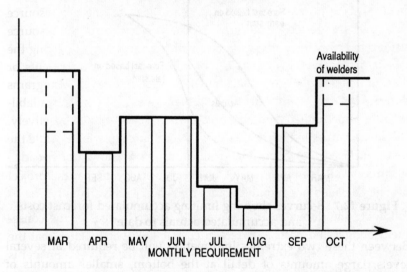

Figure 12.6 Histogram showing requirement vs availability after resource-limited schedule

Lastly, if progress payments are to be made, there will be a report of percent complete and earned value by WBS element. This report will probably consist of a simple listing for the accounts department, together with aggregated plots for comparison with the baseline for management purposes.

There are plenty of other examples of graphical depiction of plan and progress. Indeed the variation of content and style with today's computers is essentially infinite, and the important thing for the manager to know is that he can pretty well get what he wants rather than be presented with something apparently God-given that is really of no use to him.

Having dealt with the depiction of information, printed and plotted, the next step is to discuss the hierarchy of reporting. A project of any magnitude will operate at several levels. A sort of mini Grand Canyon. At the shop floor level a system will produce work orders covering periods as short as an hour, and activities as simple as "drill this hole". At the top level, say the corporate level, a report may do no more than say that this million-dollar project is on time, and that the project leader is a good chap.

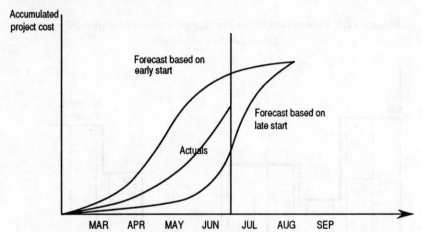

Figure 12.7 S-curves showing limiting accumulated forecast costs
and accumulated actuals to date

Between these two extremes information will be required at several levels, large amounts of detail at the bottom, smaller amounts of concentrate further up. A typical system will aggregate costs up the WBS (explicit or implicit), reporting at each level in an appropriate way and in appropriate detail. As has been the case since ancient and medieval times, the number seven has a fascination, and it seems that large projects today report at seven levels, with networks at one or pehaps two of them.

Small projects probably need only three; the network, the milestones of each individual project and an aggregation of the projects at corporate level.

Sample Output from Existing Systems

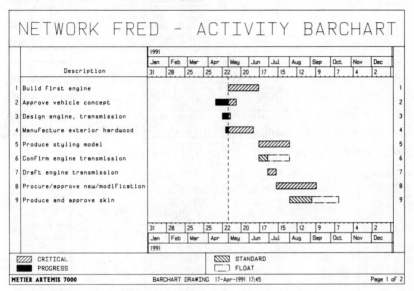

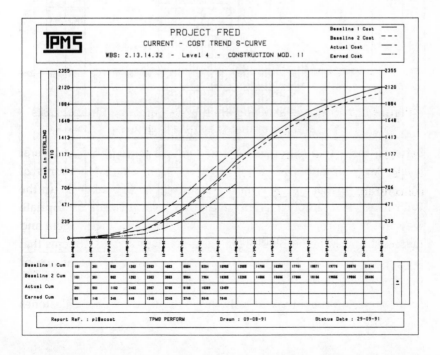

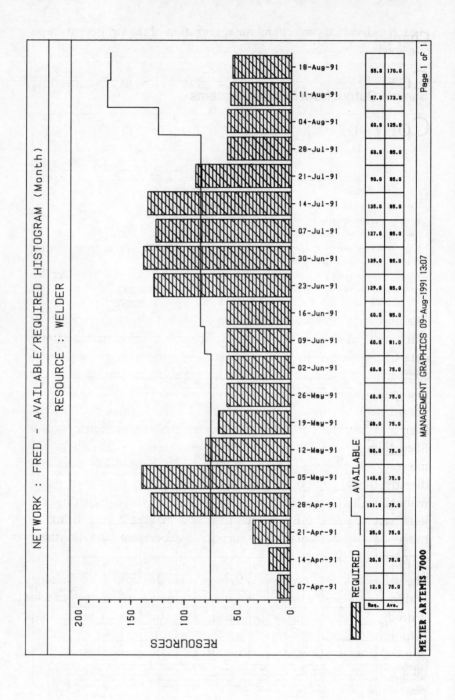

Chapter 13

Corporate Arrangements for Large Companies

Observe how System into System Runs

Alexander Pope

The burden of the preceding thoughts is that although each project will have its own plan, its own WBS and network, its own collection of data tables and its own reporting structure, it ought to be part of a company-wide structure. What has happened in the last decade is that to a great extent corporate management has let the projects down by not providing them with the computer tools to do their job. There has been a vacuum out at the projects which the project managers have filled themselves. Individual project managers, people whose only interest in computers is using them to get the job done, have gone directly to the computing industry and acquired their own project management systems. And we see companies where individual projects have acquired quite different systems making it very difficult to move data about, maximise corporate experience and do things economically.

The solution to this problem is to have a single computer technology within a company, with each individual project availing itself of what it needs. So, please, general manager, take this chapter to heart and help your project people get what they need to do your job for you. The technology will change with time, but at all times there needs to be a corporate plan to help manage that change, and the corporate plan is the GM's plan.

What should a corporate plan for project management computer technology look like? And what is so special about project management?

Why can't it be part of the total corporate plan for computing? Which again should be part of the corporate plan.

The technology will change with time

Well, to answer the last question first, most companies don't have a corporate plan for computing, and if you wait for one you will stultify the project management part. However, those companies that do have a corporate plan probably have a mechanism for including project management, and presumably use it.

Thinking now of just the project management component of the plan, the fundamental problem relates back to the discussion of the fundamental conflict between project and staff. Their immediate needs are very different. The people are different. They may be geographically miles apart; head shed in Houston, project in Saudi. There are lots of reasons why the relationship between project and staff is often not of the best. And it must be admitted that the short history of computing has not been replete with computing managers with a zeal to serve. Too often computing, sad to relate, has instead become a corporate empire, a state within a state.

But during the last décade or so the people of the project world has succeeded in bringing about a computer revolution, and in doing so has generated computer experts in their own right. It is vital, therefore, that project representation must be brought to bear on corporate decisions. This implies the existence of a corporate computing steering organ (call it a committee if you like) with project membership. It could even be that the tail wags the dog, and that because project requirements dictate such a steering committee, other interests are also included.

There also needs to be a permanent *look-ahead* function. The immediate needs of an individual project do not leave time for surveying the industry, evaluating new technology, acquiring equipment, training people etc. Moreover, the horizon of an individual project is the project itself. It doesn't have the extra budget, and it has no responsibility for projects to follow. Projects come to a close, teams disband, equipment gets reassigned; there is no continuity and no possibility of a long-term view. Inevitably this is a staff function.

The consequence of a viable look-ahead function will be decisions on equipment, people, training etc. Call this the *provision* function.

The task of the provision function is to provide each project with all the computing requirements. A narrow view of this would be just a computer and a chunk of software. But that isn't enough. There may be no one on the project itself with the detailed knowledge of how to use it, nor the time nor inclination to learn. Most projects are behind the gun right from the start. The broad view would be a complete computing *cell*; hardware, software, communication lines, a database of relevant corporate information, a system designer/implementer, or team, perhaps some trained terminal operators. What the project manager wants is a bunch of plumbers who know how to plumb, a crane, a warm, dry shack, and a competent computer team to carry out his orders. He gets the plumbers, the crane and the shack, but there's hardly a project manager anywhere in the world who gets the computer team.

This has to change, and it is starting to do so. The technology is now in place, and it is now only a question of corporate awareness and resolve.

The total provision function contains a number of discrete subordinate functions, as follows:

1. *System overview*

   Firstly it must maintain a detailed knowledge of the computer systems currently in use, and must act as a responsive consultant to the immediate needs of current projects. But in solving current problems it becomes aware of evolving needs, and thereby has a target against which to measure the effectiveness of current systems. The difference provides the impetus for looking at future versions of current systems and at competitive systems.

2. *Resources*

Secondly it must maintain a plan for computing resources. This isn't easy because no one wants to commit expenditure against a project until the dotted line is signed. A project management plan is therefore different to a staff plan in that you cannot guarantee to get a project. At best it must be based on probabilities. The problem is that when a project does go live it needs the resources immediately. So the reality is that the provision function has to know how it can obtain resources quickly, and this in practice usually means sharing equipment already being used by other projects.

We often see in companies today several projects using the same equipment, fighting for resources, with no one solidly in charge. A central provision function solves these problems equally for everyone, and removes another problem, that of the relationship with the computer supplier.

3. *Maintenance*

Thus the third provision function is maintenance, a service normally carried out by the supplier. Computer maintenance contracts should be made corporately. It means that the project has only one phone number to ring, that of the provision function, whatever the problem, hardware, software, communications. And it helps the supplier provide a better service in that he has one large customer rather than several small ones to deal with and can thereby rationalise parts and staff better.

4. *Awareness and training*

The fourth function is awareness and training. When a new project comes into being it may well be that the manager and his immediate staff don't know what is available. They may be new altogether to the use of computers, or their knowledge is based on an earlier system or version. So early on in the life of the project a dialogue has to take place between staff and project, initiated by the awareness function, but leading to a set of requirements and the consequent training.

What is immediately available depends largely on what preceding projects have done; what applications they have generated and used. Can the new project use existing applications or are the details so different that they have to start from scratch? Or can existing applications be modified?

5. *New applications*

   The key to success of today's project management computer systems is the speed with which an experienced programmer can create a new program. Traditionally, with by now ancient computing languages, computing departments take months and even years to create systems for people. Perhaps some kinds of organisation can afford to wait that long. Not projects. Projects need results now. Or forget it. Days, perhaps weeks, not months or years.

   With top-quality people and a good computer tool, the implementation function can do its job within allowable project timeframes. But those people must be instantly available. It must not be the project's responsibility to train them.

6. *Quality assurance*

   The sixth function is that of quality assurance. Does the new application work? Does it contain bugs? Is it likely to lose all the data the day after it's all been input? Is it easy to use? Does the manager have to be a computer expert to run it? The trouble with QA is that there's no science to it. There is no theorem to prove that a computer program works; that it will work correctly in all circumstance. This means the existence of people who somehow have that certain instinct for finding them. A QA function will not find all the bugs. Only daily, real-life experience can do that, but a good QA function will do most of the job and provide the users with something that works most of the time.

7. *Documentation*

   Experience shows that there are very few organisations that understand the need for documentation, or seem to be able to produce it. But how can you train people without it? How can a would-be user know what a system contains or how to get at it without some form of description and explanation? How can a programmer produce enhancements to an application if there is no technical documentation explaining how it works, how the data tables relate, the screen forms etc? Again, the projects cannot be expected to produce much documentation, but they certainly need it, and it has to be the responsibility of the provision function to provide it.

This more or less summarises the components of the computer-aided project management provision function; its activities feed up into the corporate plan, which is the working paper of the steering committee and the look-ahead function. In a small company there will be more functions than people, but in a large one a viable corporate staff might be fairly large. Whichever, its existence needs to be clearly recognised and well staffed and managed.

Chapter 14

Arrangements for Small Companies

Si Parva Licet Componere Magnis
(If One May Compare Small Things With Great)

Virgil, 1st. Century B.C.

A typical large project consists of a thousand activities lasting in total three or four years, involving between five hundred and a thousand people, and costing perhaps several hundred million dollars. Such a project would have a planning team, say five people, backed up by one or two full-time programmers. The planning system would require at least a minicomputer of a thousand megabytes capacity, or even a large mainframe computer. This would be particularly true if the data needed and created by the planning system tied in automatically with other systems used by the project, for example computer-aided design, purchasing and salaries.

By contrast a typical small project consists of about a hundred activities lasting about a year, involving between ten and a hundred people, and costing perhaps as little as a million dollars. The initial planning might take only half a day, and the planner might need only a few hours a month to report progress. Thanks to the rapid development of the personal computer of both camps, IBM and Apple, there is plenty of capacity at rock-bottom prices to house these projects. And plenty of systems to choose from. So how should the small company set about it? What are the similarities and differences between large and small companies? Again, big or small, the general manager should be well aware of what his project people need.

To start to answer these questions let me digress for a moment to make an important point. During the four decades of the computing era there has been an inevitable specialisation on the part of computer programmers. When it all started the applications were of necessity so simple that anyone who could master the Byzantian intricacies of the computer hardware and logic could write the necessary programs. But as computer memories got large, and linguistic techniques evolved, specialised languages developed to enable programmers to write much more efficiently - and to write much more efficient programs (not at all the same thing). This in turn led to a progressively broader range of specialisation, way beyond the simple adding up of numbers. This has meant that within a single company, even a large one, it has become progressively more expensive to employ a computing department capable of everything. Observing this problem we see a mushrooming of software companies specialising in particular applications. These companies are capable of far better software than computer departments traditionally produce, the reason being the richer experience provided them by their customers. And they are cheaper by virtue of the fact that they do it once and sell it again and again (with the slight modification).

This all leads up to the question of whether a company should own a computing department, and if so what its function should be. My advice, having lived through it all, is as follows. A large company should most certainly have a computing department, but it should no longer write programs. Its staff should consist of computer project managers; perhaps has-been programmers with a flair for management and a solid knowledge of their company. Their job is to select an appropriate supplier for a particular application, write the specification, negotiate the contract, wring a plan from the contractor, bird-dog the project, not forgetting its quality assurance phase, and then ensure a healthy follow-up maintenance function. This is the key to the successful obtaining of large computer programs after nearly half a century of evolution. I would even include the operations of the large computers. Indeed, I would also farm out the computer capacity. I would rather share a larger machine with a richer array of software than have a smaller one all to myself.

So much for the large company. What does the smaller company need? Well, the very minimum for a company that uses personal computers of the IBM world is a full-time expert in the operating system. Experience dictates that you simply cannot function unless you have someone roaming your corridors who is able to provide a perambulating service to the rest of the employees. The IBM world is replete with incompatibility. Standards are so important that everybody has his own. There are different disk sizes and recording densities. Some 3.5 inch disks have two holes in the corners, and others only one. There is no standard way of taking advantage of the memory to improve speed. No standard system of displaying the contents of the machine. And everybody makes printers, but no one has yet solved the problem of loading paper into them satisfactorily.

The problem with the PC is the adjective. It is very difficult to convince an employee that the computer sitting on his desk or on his lap is not absolutely personal; his own private property. So he goes ahead and, by the Great Universal Mystery of the late twentieth century, acquires programs to help him do his job. The argument that his job isn't personal, but is part of a grander design, doesn't seem to carry much weight. Or management doesn't appear to understand the problem and therefore doesn't pontificate upon the subject.

And having once obtained his software he then requires the instant intervention of the peripatetic PC expert to rescue him from his inevitable disasters.

As an aside to this digression it is germane to point out that all this makes for an interesting world. There is a global masonry of DOS experts out there. And you are welcome with your catastrophe wherever you go. (DOS is Microsoft's Disk Operating System; certainly the world's most heard-of computer program.) My current job takes me to the most outlandish places, and I have to grapple with DOS in German, Danish, French and Finnish. But I have been rescued from disk unreadability and had paper successfully inserted into my printer by Bombay Indians in Bahrain with kindness, courtesy and an impressive knowledge of mysteries dossian.

But back to the digression. So the very minimum the most minimal of organisations needs is a hot-shot DOS prop, and it is tempting to imagine him doubling as the planning system expert (though not as the planner). The only problem with this arrangement is that he probably wouldn't have time to provide the planning support. While you were trying to do your monthly progress update there would be a crisis with the payroll program. Better to have an engineer with a modicum of keyboard dexterity to learn the planning system.

On the other hand the world of the Apple MacIntosh doesn't seem to require computer experts to anything like the same degree as IBM. Programs seem to work the first time, and you don't need to be a computer expert to install them or keep them going. So a small organisation with Apple at its core can probably manage without a single computer specialist. In that case the planning system specialist has no choice but be seconded from an existing department. (At the time of writing, the Windows software and its inevitable successors seem to be closing the gap between the two PC worlds, and may well put some of the DOS consultants out of a job.)

The rest of the digression can be found in the Appendix; a deeper discussion of the relative roles of computers, personal and impersonal.

How to decide? Who will learn the system? The easy answer is that there is so much choice, so much competition, that it doesn't much matter. At least to start with. Both schools of PC have project systems available, and they are cheap. The important thing is to make the initial decision to plan properly and use the plans to help you run your organisation.

However, after you have spent two or three years gaining experience you may be concerned about the limitations of your chosen system. No matter. There is plenty you can do about it. There are basically two types of system, closed and open. The closed systems are immutable except that every other year or two the supplier (if he's still in business) issues a new version containing features that large numbers of potential customers appear to need. The new version may or may not satisfy your particular requirements. If it doesn't you can at least content yourself with the fact that you didn't pay much for it.

An open system is one that allows you to change it at will. An open system contains a language that is accessible to you, and after learning that language you can use it to elaborate your system to satisfy very precise needs. An open system will cost you more (but not much more). However, cost is not the real problem. Rather it is the problem of learning and using the underlying language. My advice is never try. You will almost certainly get side-tracked away from project management over to computer programming. Better to contract a specialist company to do it for you. You will pay more, but you will get what you really want, and this may be vital to your success when you become a knowledgeable project manager. By then you will have to learn enough about the economics to be able to compare cost with value.

So, in summary, the small company would be best to buy a very simple, cheap system, appropriate to the PC already in use. Use it whenever possible, and learn from experience what I have tried to describe in this book - enough to know what you really need. A simple system should be very easy to wrench yourself away from, and you should not suffer the problem of people's reluctance to learn new tricks. A hand-sculpted system, while necessarily containing more features than one off the shelf, should nevertheless be just as easy to use. Everything is done from menus. No operator skill required, and almost no training manual. The menus simply get steadily longer as you add new features.

A variation of the small company is the large company that consists of a number of geographically spread small subsidiaries. In this case the project planning system should be supplied from corporate headquarters, a single source ensuring commonality. The same discussion holds as with the simple small company except that an additional export-import feature would be required for sending plans on disk from one company to another, and between companies and headquarters. Sending disks by Datapost is cheap and reliable. Datapost and telefax make an excellent company communications system.

What also characterises the small company is that it often runs many projects in parallel. Each individual project will have its own start and finish dates, and at any point in time there will typically be a spectrum of progress. Some will have just begun, with their usual scramble for resources, others will be in mid-stream, occupying most of management's attention, while there is hope that some are in their final death throes, their managers looking forward to taking a pile of accumulated leave.

Large companies, of course, run projects in parallel, but normally run them as water-tight organisations, each with its dedicated office, staff and computer. The special problem with small companies is that they cannot afford such luxuries. They are forced to oscillate people back and forth between projects, often with bewildering frequency, and are restricted to a single computer on which to run all the projects. But the latter is not necessarily a problem. Indeed it can be an advantage. You can comfortably house ten or twenty projects on ten megabytes of storage, ie on a fraction of today's PC. The advantage is that you can keep the total resource details in a single database, allowing you to allocate them as required, without passing data from one computer to another, providing each employee with his personal plan, independent of project. A single planner can keep track of all the individual projects and run them as a single logical project.

And here we come to a vital fundamental idea; the Key to Reduced Bewilderment. Please hang this illustration on your office wall.

Never believe anything produced on a typewriter

If plans are made by hand, and people's instructions imparted via typewriter, you have a guarantee of conflict. People will be double parked and worse. If, on the other hand, all instructions come from a single planning database, they will be consistent. There will be a single version of the truth. There will be no possibility of a resource being assigned to two activities at the same time. To the extent that the plans are good the resource allocations will be sensible.

You will never eliminate bewilderment. But you can reduce it to a minimum. If the instructions come off a computer printer they are probably valid, even though they sometimes contain an element of mystery. If they come off a typewriter they probably aren't.

The final step in the remorseless chain of logic for the small company is this. All the company's projects are planned on a single computer, and this will probably comprise most of what the company is currently engaged in. At least its creative endeavours. In other words, the totality of the project plans becomes the company plan. The project leader of the company plan of action is no less than the company general manager. In other words, the monthly project review is in reality the monthly corporate review. And who better to run the meeting than the general manager? He might learn a lot about his own company if he did, and he might learn a lot about management. He need only review the critical activities. There won't be many of these to detain him long at the meeting, but they could well give him a goodly chunk of his agenda for the coming four weeks.

Management is the management of detail. Successful management is the management of the right details. These are all depicted in red, governor. You have it handed to you on a plate. At last, a prescription for good management. All you've ever wanted. The cost of the system is peanuts. Its value is the value of the company - if you take the simple decision to make it so.

As a postscript one could say that large companies could be managed in exactly the same way, with a single logical database comprising the disparate physical databases. However, I think we'll have to await a generation change before there is much hope of this. It is no longer a technical problem. It is a problem of attitude. Managers of very large companies traditionally distance themselves from the detail, and instead play the take-over game as a substitute for individual profitability. They have to do something with their time I suppose.

This chapter has tried to describe a modus operandi for the small company. Details concerning costs are sketched out in the next chapter.

You will never eliminate bewilderment

Chapter 15

But What is it All Worth?

Take thy Bill, and Sit Down Quickly, and Write Fifty

Gospel According to St. Luke

Having discussed the technology and hopefully convinced you that you dare not embark upon any more projects without a good computer tool at your elbow, you will naturally want to know how to get started and how much you can expect to spend. What systems are there available? On what computers? Which one is the right one for me? Where do I get it from? How do I learn how to use it? What equipment do I need? How do I integrate it with any current systems? How much will it all cost? I hope that these questions are now uppermost in your mind.

Although this chapter discusses technical questions, it is ultimately about cost and value, and the general manager should at least be aware of the value of using computers - for project management as well as any other application.

One problem that you will have is that there are now a fair number of planning and control systems on the market, and the number is growing. The main reason for this is that the capacity of the personal computer has become impressively great, allowing for considerable sophistication. Today's PC is much bigger than the minicomputer of a decade ago, when this technology started life.

There are several immediate factors, possibly conflicting, that you will need to bear in mind, and together they serve to emphasise some of the key points made in the preceding chapters. Here is a short list:

1. *Existing situation*

   Most companies already have computer equipment and a running system containing databases and user programs. Normally a great deal of investment has gone into the computer complex, including the training of people and establishment of company procedures. If at all possible, any new system should fit in smoothly with the existing systems so that from the user's point of view it is simply an extension of what he or she is already used to. This is particularly true for planning and control systems because they need information from existing systems and provide information to those systems. The only circumstances in which intrusive new equipment should be considered is one in which there is no planning and control system available for the existing equipment or where available software is considered to be either too expensive or inadequate.

2. *Price range*

The cheapest planning system costs under $1,000 and the most expensive over $100,000. There is a fair choice at the $10,000 to $15,000 level, but at the moment an empty gap from there to the $100,000 level. They are available on large mainframe computers and on some minis (eg Hewlett Packard 1000 and Digital Equipment's VAX machines), but the main development is taking place on the PC, hence the low price of some of the systems. But don't be afraid of low prices. In the world of the PC there are no well-established guidelines for price and value. Some of the cheap planning systems are really quite good. Moreover, whatever the basic price, if additional copies were to be purchased what sort of discount would you get?

3. *Features*

The central core of necessary features is found in most of today's available planning packages. This comprises the following:

- Creation of WBS and networks
- Specification of resources
- Specification of calendars
- Network analysis
- Network scheduling
- Reporting, printed and plotted

Beyond this are central features that are not included in all packages. These are primarily concerned with building up a database and attaching a growing set of user-programs to it; the ability to evolve systems as you gain experience.

4. *Ease of use*

One of the most important developments in computers continues to be that of the user interface. As we said at the end of

Chapter 5, there is always something newer on the shelf than what we have on the desk. We have seen miraculous improvements in the ability of the user to get to grips with the programs, and by now most of the fear of the unknown has been swept away along with difficulty of accessing data and processing it. If you want a manager to plan, at least make it easy for him. A computer tool that almost reads his mind will win over one that forces him to learn to play the organ. So, whatever else you consider, choose a system that gives fingertip response from within the network for as much of the planning as possible.

5. *Closed type systems*

   The *closed* type of system (defined in the preceding chapter) restricts you to selecting options from fixed menus. Almost all closed packages contain networking, while some contain an explicit WBS function, though few seem to contain both. However, since it is possible to code the network to create an *implicit* WBS, together with the ability to aggregate to progressively higher levels, it is always possible to create a complete system from a networking-only package. The reverse is not true, however, because a WBS-only package does not contain activity dependency. The fundamental problem with the closed type of system is that you are constrained to operate within a rigid framework provided by the menus. On the other hand, closed systems are very easy to learn.

6. *Open type systems*

   The *open* type of system allows you much greater freedom than the closed. You are provided with a language that you can use either to manipulate data on the fly, as the need arises, or to create menus of your own for use by your people according to their requirements. While a language requires orders of magnitude more learning than a set of menus, the payoff from the investment is the freedom to tailor systems that truly match your requirements.

7. *Integrability*

   Following from section 1, if a new type of hardware is needed to carry the selected package, it is important that its database can be linked via communication lines to the existing company equipment, and that data can be transferred effortlessly between the planning system and the existing systems. This should be done in a way that is invisible to the user.

8. *Multi-user*

   An important consideration is whether the planning and control systems shall be single or multi-user. Most of the current packages allow only one user to have access to a database; each user has his own more or less private data world. This has proved to be a distinct problem. In most practical cases the using company wants to operate a single database, allowing any user to access whatever data he is entitled to, whenever he needs to. It is vital to ask this question and to understand the answer.

9. *Size and growth*

It may be difficult at first to predict how much use a planning and control system might get, how complex each application might become, how large the networks might become, and how large the database. No one wants to pay for more than he needs, so it is important that a user is able to start cheaply, but can expand the size and scope of his equipment and software according to need. Inevitably the need will increase beyond his original estimates, but that isn't sufficient grounds for paying a high price before he is sure that the value is there.

10. *Game-playing*

Once a plan has been made, beyond its use as the basis for managing the project, it can be used as a simulation tool. By making experimental changes to the plan one may explore alternatives to predict the consequences of changed circumstances. What would happen if ...? A good system lends itself easily to this kind of game-playing. Moreover, since this is mainly of interest to senior management, often people with very little fluency with computers, it is vital that this is made easy.

11. *Research and development*

A particular game that is not at all easy to play is planning R&D projects. By the very nature of research you cannot predict durations with any degree of precision. The best you can do is hope. But hope is the salt of R&D. Without it we wouldn't even try. A plan based on hope is better than no plan at all, and you can temper hope with a modicum of statistics by guessing the hopeless. A system that allows you to estimate optimistic and pessimistic durations, and subject them to a Monte Carlo analysis, provides the basis for R&D planning. And as a footnote to this section it should be pointed out that there is a sort of political difference between research and development. In Chapter 3 we differentiated between closed and open planning. If research is carried out on some sort of grant it is by definition closed. When your time is up your money runs out and you have to write up your results, if you have any. Development, on the other hand, is open. You are supposed to make something, and the project keeps on until either you succeed or your successor succeeds.

12. *Supplier solidity*

In all probability a user, once he has started to invest substantial amounts of money and training in a particular package, will want to live with that package and its possible improvements for a fair period of time. Does the purchase of a package bring with it a guarantee of periodic improvements? How is it decided what those improvements will be? How much influence has the individual customer over future development? How big a development staff does the supplier have? How well established is the supplier? How many customers are there? Does the package and its supplier have a future? Will they still be around five years from now?

13. *Assistance*

The above are some of the main criteria to observe while evaluating project planning and control systems. However, probably the most important point to make is that there are plenty of people around who have already made all the mistakes, and they can be consulted to help prevent a newcomer repeating them. Performing an investigation before choosing a system usually pays dividends, and the first investigation should be to determine whether or not one has problems that are soluble by traditional planning and control techniques.

Having said all that, probably the best advice to give would be to start simply and build carefully. So perhaps ease of use, and certainly cheapness, might be more important at the start than integrability; closed rather than open. Use a simple cheap system to experiment and learn; something that you could cheerfully discard later on when you start down the one-way road to an integrated system.

... start simply and build carefully

So start with a cheap, simple PC system. Choose a software package that is so simple to use that you don't have to learn anything. No instruction book. Failing that, a system whose instruction book is built in. You need to be quickly blooded. You need to be able to knock up a network of thirty activities without any consideration of resources, report formats or menus. This will give you confidence and will throw up a short list of questions the answers to which will help you add a few features to the bare network to create the glimmering of a system. This will be followed by another round of questions and a further layer to the system. Learn by playing. Learn by intuition.

Gradually add to the network five or ten activities at a time so that your model approaches reality and begins to describe the project you are working on. All the initial constraints can be finish-to-start, but after a while you can make things more realistic by introducing other types of constraint and embellishing these with delay estimates. Concerning resources, start with only one resource per activity, then add other resources to those activities which require them and watch the effect on the dates.

When you have evolved a fair approximation to reality, even though you may not yet put the system to productive use, monitor it closely and gain confidence. Eventually, if all goes well, you will reach the stage where you are quite sure it works and can begin to entrust your operations to the reports it produces.

At this stage you will have become sufficiently knowledgeable to be able to make an intelligent decision as to what kind of system really suits your needs. Either you will be satisfied with your first choice of software - lucky you - or you will know enough to be able to undertake a survey of available packages, this time more strongly guided by the factors listed above, an important goal being to integrate the new system into your existing panoply of accounting, billing, ordering, payroll etc. systems. A few guidelines are provided in the next chapter.

From that point on it is only a question of making the best use possible of the basic software, learning by experience, and ensuring that the project people at all times have a profitable tool at their disposal.

I said that you can acquire a package for under $1,000, but you can also pay $100,000, so we should now discuss the question of benefit in some detail.

As soon as you start talking about project management systems people naturally ask, how much do they cost? Or even, sorry I can't afford one. The small company looks at the offshore industry and feels immediately intimidated. It's OK for those big companies. They can afford it. I'm too small.

Perhaps small companies think that big companies don't care about the cost of things. In actual practice the converse is true. The bigger the company the bigger the bill and the greater the number of potential critics.

Large companies, to stay large, must be just as cost-conscious as small ones. And small companies, if they were even more cost-conscious than they are, could perhaps become large companies.

Of course, it isn't a question of cost in isolation, it's a question of profitability. What it costs against what it is worth. So, before you can usefully talk about costs of new ideas you have to have some idea of what it is costing you today. The problem is that most companies don't have much feel for what it might cost if they were to do it differently. So they don't have much basis for discussing how much they might be willing to pay.

So, to discuss costs intelligently we have to start with what it is costing today, and what the saving might be over a given period of time, say three years.

What is the lack of structured and systematic project management costing you today? The following is a list of components to examine in answering that question:

1. *Late finish*

   The overall value of any project management system is that it helps you meet your deadlines. It gives you better warning of the parts of the project that are potentially behind schedule, helping you to prevent delays actually happening. So what has late delivery cost you in the past?

   Late delivery probably costs you a contractual penalty. It certainly results in an over-run on labour costs. It leads to delayed starts on following projects because of the unavailability of people, and it can lead to rumours in the market place.

   Some of those costs are tangible, and available from the company accountant. Others are intangible, and are only available from the salesmen who find themselves up against credibility problems with new hoped-for customers.

2. *Poor estimating*

   Homo sapiens has survived solely on optimism. If he had known what was in store for him he would have never left the cave. If realistic estimates had been made, very little of mankind's achievements would have seen the light of day; certainly not the Sydney Opera House. But it's not your job to build monuments, so you must recognise the fundamental component of mankind's make-up, optimism, and treat all estimates with suspicion. Base the future systematically on the past.

   A growing value of a project management system is that it enables you automatically to build up an experience databank. At the completion of each project the system contains exact figures of time and money spent on every activity. In each succeeding project it is then possible to make much better estimates than before, hence more accurate total costs, and hence greater profitability.

   So what has poor estimating cost you in the past? You may have finished on time, but it cost you more on the way than you had bargained for, and you didn't make as much on the project as you had hoped.

3. *Bad timing*

   The best time to deliver anything to the site is exactly when it is needed; people, materials and equipment. Late delivery leads to either a late finish or extra costs (overtime) to make up for lost time. Early delivery means unnecessary investment in materials and the possibility of corruption by moth and dust.

   So how much has bad timing cost you in the past? How good

have you been at receiving and delivering exactly what you've needed as you need it? How much do you lose each year from damaged or stolen property?

4. *Inadequate resources*

   Systematic planning forces you to think more carefully about the resources you need, expecially human resources. The lack of a single man can cause overtime and can mean an entire team having to wait before it can even start on an activity. The lack of a crane driver for example. How often has this happened to you? How often has bad planning led to insufficient manpower to carry out a job? And what has this cost?

5. *Overmanning*

   The converse. How often has bad planning led to idle hands? And what has this cost?

6. *Both (the big company problem)*

   And, worst of all, how often have you experienced too many men on one job and too few on another, just because proper work orders hadn't been prepared. And worse still, how often have you had idle hands on one site and hired-in contractors on another? And what has all this cost?

7. *Slow start*

   You signed the contract, the customer was expecting immediate action but nothing apparently happened. The reason for this is that a lot of what should have happened before you signed happened afterwards. If the bid contained a plan, understood and supported by the management team, you could start carrying out that plan as soon as the light went green. Instead, what usually happens is that you get the contract (big surprise) and have to run around getting organised instead of actually producing anything.

   The first activity in any plan is to produce the plan itself. Better to do this before obtaining the contract than afterwards. A late start often leads to the entire project lying behind schedule with consequent pressure throughout. In turn this leads to bad workmanship, rework and all stations to unprofitability.

   How good are you at getting started on time? And how much have late starts cost you? Be honest now. We are all sinners.

8. *The cost of planning*

   In the autumn of 1958 I produced a planning system on a very small computer that in eight minutes per month did the job of a ten-men planning department. We are now three decades and umpteen computer generations further on, and there ought no longer to be such things as planning departments - at least not large ones. How much is planning costing you today? What are the planners doing? What could they be doing that might be more useful?

9. *The cost of replanning*

It is relatively easy to make the first version of a plan. There is time enough waiting for the customer to make up his mind. The problem is that of replanning suddenly in the middle of the project. And often. You need the new version immediately and there isn't time to do it properly. You resort to guesswork, and the reworked plan is a disaster.

How often do you find yourself replanning? What does it cost you to make the revised plan? And how much does the resulting disaster cost you?

10. *Involving the customer*

Does the customer appear in your plans? Is he responsible for some of the activities? Is he supposed to have premises ready for you to install the equipment? How often has he sabotaged your projects by being late himself? How much has this cost you? How easy was it to remonstrate with him (with the future in mind)? If the plan is part of the contract, with his activities coloured pink, he can show up at the review meetings, you can keep an eye on his progress, and, despite your excellent management, if he does cause a delay the remonstration will consist of the silent pointing of your pipe to the network. You don't have to smoke it (the pipe). An almost imperceptible sucking sound will do the trick.

Well, these are some of the important sources of profit locked up in bad planning. Have a good heart-search first. Try to estimate what it is costing you each year that a decent system could help you avoid. There's your value.

And given the value of a system, how much are you willing to pay to have one? One year's saving? Three years? How long might you be able to live with the first version? How much might you have to spend in evolving something that would really do the job?

It will cost you something even to find out accurately what bad planning is costing you today. So, to bypass that activity to begin with, the following orders of magnitude are worth considering:

Does the customer appear in your plans?

A company with an annual turnover of $100 million can expect to make a profit of about $15 million. Suppose the cost of bad planning were 1% of this, the value of a system would be $150,000 per annum. If you already have a personal computer you would have that much to spend on a system of your own. With a basic package of $10,000 you would have enough left over for a month's development work, and this could well be enough. On the other hand, if the cost of bad planning were 5% the value of the system would be $750,000 p.a. This would give you plenty of scope for system development.

A company with an annual turnover of only $10 million would have to be making heavy losses from bad planning to justify a similar investment in a planning system. On the other hand, the value of such a system for bidding purposes, for increasing the business, might well justify a similar investment of $150,000. One extra job could well pay for it.

In the other direction, anything over $100 million turnover implies a possible investment that could create a very usable system. As a postscript to the discussion of value, consider the value of using a system to secure more work; computer-aided competition.

A project really starts at the bid stage. When you sign a contract you have to have a very clear idea of what it is you are signing; what the job is all about, how long it is going to take, what resources it will need, how much it will cost, and above all who is going to run it. A lot of work goes into producing a bid, and you can only get it right if at the centre of it all there is a detailed plan; indeed, the plan you will actually use if you get the job.

Computer-aided competition

Since you need the plan to do the job, why not use it to *get* the job? Firstly prove to yourself that you know what you are doing, and then prove it to the hoped-for customer. There is nothing more convincing than a detailed network, backed up by the other graphical byproducts. Not only are you then in a position to hold a detailed discussion with the customer, one in which you will be in the driving seat, but you are also seen by him to have done your homework.

There are several valuable spin-offs from using the computer already at the bid stage:

1. Bids are expensive. Nobody scores 100%, and companies of necessity try to optimise the situation and achieve as high a score as possible with as little investment as possible. A good bid system, based as much as possible on corporate experience and a current facilities load database, ought to be able to produce bid material much faster and at much less cost than by hand and memory, and give you much better protection against bad estimating.

2. You may be bidding in a consortium with one or more other companies. Group bidding is a time-consuming process, the networks never match up and it's often difficult to find out who's in charge. If you all have bidding systems you can let the bidding

systems do most of the work; quick and cheap. If you have one and the others don't it helps you gain control. Either way, you have a much better idea before you go in what the other members of the consortium are contracting to do, so you know where you stand.

3. You may frighten the customer. Your price may be way higher than he had expected. You may come in much higher than the competition. Why does it cost so much? Is it really going to take that long? You are doing both the customer and yourself a bad service to provide low estimates. Even if you are the high bidder, if you back up your bid with solid data, presented in an assimilable way, you will carry conviction and win the day. It is the low bidder who then looks suspicious. Where is his network? What's missing from it? Has he done his homework properly?

These are some of the advantages of investing in a bidding system, but perhaps the most important is that of being certain yourself of what you are letting yourself in for when you sign a contract.

That completes our discussion of costs and values, and it only remains now to take the plunge.

Chapter 16

Getting Going

Where Shall I Begin Please Your Majesty?

Lewis Carroll

Having convinced you that you can't live without a planning and control system, and that you can afford one, let us conclude by proffering some advice; what to look for in the basic software of a system, what equipment you might need and how you might set about it.

This chapter should be the basis of a discussion between the general manager, his project managers and his computer people. Invest some time together before taking the plunge. But the subject is how, not whether.

As we have just said, a great deal depends on how big your company is, how big the projects it handles, how many and how long they last, how widely spread your operations geographically, and so on. So it is very difficult to generalise.

The minimum usable computer today is a 20 megabyte PC, although a PS2 with 120 megabytes is so cheap and fast that it is difficult to recommend anything less. There is a glut of printers on the market from which you can take your pick. You don't have to have a plotter, and the choice is fairly limited (a good thing really). However, they are remarkably reliable, they come in all sizes and are becoming quite fast. The point about a plotter is not that it allows you to portray more information than a black and white printed plot, but that coloured pictures are much easier to read to the casual observer - your boss or your customers. As the Chinese will tell you, the best place to put information is on the wall. And it needs to be eye-catching to achieve its effect.

In the middle range are the minicomputers. The machine that has led the world in the development of the technology is the HP1000, although this is now in process of being replaced by much more powerful equipment. Also in the mini range are the SUN, VAX and Prime machines.

At the top end, of course, are the IBM mainframes and equivalent machines, providing software of the capacity needed by the very largest users.

What is becoming extremely important is the ability to move data fluently between computers, in particular between PCs and central computers, making it possible to marry project databases with corporate databases, as discussed in Chapter 10. This necessitates good communications hardware and software, and more or less necessitates the possibility of several users having access to the database; a multiuser system.

An important early decision is whether you and your people will become expert in creating systems or whether you will content yourselves with specifying requirements, letting a specialist implement them for you. The advantage with the former is that to the extent that your own people don't quit to become consultants you retain the expertise in house. The advantage with the latter is that you will get better implementations earlier than doing it yourself - and you can insist on documentation, something you never get from your own employees.

If you decide to let specialists do the work, the details of the software aren't of much concern provided you get the system you have specified, and within budget. On the other hand if you do it yourself you will be very interested in the software, so let us review some of the more important features that you need to consider.

Everything starts at the screen, be it a PC or a terminal. The screen is the mirror of the soul of the computer. A friendly, fluent screen probably means a friendly, fluent system inside the machine. You want menus and windows popping up and down like Monty Python's dancing teeth.

A screen should be as pictorial as possible, requiring a minimum of verbal interaction. It shouldn't be necessary to know how to spell. All the coding, program structure, syntax and other manifestations of computer technology should be hidden behind the pictures. The database might contain millions of items of information, and there may be a wide range of operations performed on them. But it must be trivially easy to window in on what interests you at a particular point in time. You should not have to play arpeggios on the keyboard. A quick flick of a single key or a mouse should be adequate to set an intense flurry of computing activity going. You should expect rapid response most of the time. You will soon learn which processes take time.

It might be interesting to interpolate a word here about what actually does go on behind the scenes. The computer wasn't born yesterday. It has taken forty years of development of both hardware and software to bring you the power, ease and comfort of today's computer. Computers have become such simple things, at least as seen by the user. In actual fact the inner complexity is almost beyond description. But that shouldn't surprise anyone. The human mind and body are orders of magnitude even more complex. It seems a relatively easy matter to scratch your head, but the chemical-electrical-nervous-muscular-mechanical system that makes this possible is still far from being properly understood.

It seems a relatively easy matter to
scratch your head

A couple of examples of the hidden complexity are the modern relational database, and automatic network plotting. The former was twenty years in coming. Today I can, on a whim, ask an unpremeditated question; how much overtime was worked last week on activity 52 by welders over 30 years of age, married with one child? Even ten years ago this was more or less unthinkable. The answer may pop out within the minute, and the process will appear to be trivial. But it isn't. It takes a very complicated data structure, and a complicated attached process to do it, the result of years of experimentation by some very bright people. The true cost of bringing you that answer is incalculable.

While database technology has been a development engaged in by lots of people around the world, producing masses of learned publications, network plotting has been developed in lighthouses, but again by some very clever people. In this case there has been little published, and one fears that there has been a lot of duplicated effort. Whereas database technology lends itself fairly well to objective description, network plotting, for all its apparent visibility, doesn't. The problem is that of quality. What makes a good picture? What are the criteria of a good placement and routing algorithm? To what extent do you want to keep the picture stable as you add activities? Do you want to group activities with like resources? Even if this means a wild spaghetti-like arrangement of constraints? Not easy to get people to agree. Nevertheless, today's network plot routines are good. Try producing better plots by hand!

The network itself should be easy to draw on the screen. It should be easy to input activity information and to add the constraints. The main problem with networks is seeing the whole picture. You cannot get more than about a dozen activities on the screen, ten percent, one percent or even less of the entire network, so it must be very easy to move your window around the network. In the same vein, since you really don't want too many activities at any one level in the network, it should be an easy matter to group activities into subnets.

In Chapter 11 we talked about menus. If you are creating a system for someone else to use you will want to provide the user with a well-structured menu mechanism. This must be easy to arrange. And once you've done it, only you should be able to get in behind the scenes and change it. Some of today's software packages suffer from the fact that they aren't lockable. You spend three months creating a system for a customer, elegantly documented, exactly according to prescription. The next day one of his computer freaks decides to improve it beyond all recognition. The map no longer agrees with the terrain, his changes by-pass the calculation module, everything shows up 100% complete and your phone rings with an unwelcome stridence.

Having made solid arrangements for inputting data you will want it regurgitated in the form of a report. Should the package provide standard report formats or provide you with the means of making your own? While the actual WBS and network information, dates, quantities, elapsed times etc, may well lend themselves to standard formats, the same cannot generally be said for the outer rings of information. A good system will make it easy for you to create your own report formats, while perhaps providing some standards for you to use in the early stages while your main attention is still more on content than appearance.

The agglomoration of hardware, software, application and communications together constitute a planner's work station. But this isn't enough. The work station should be made part of a planning and control centre, a windowless room equipped for holding project review meetings. This implies plenty of wall space for displaying graphical portrayals of progress, and on-line projectors for interactive group use of the systems.

But above all the key to a successful start is the right person. If you can find the right person all else will follow. The purpose of this book is to try to convince you that there is a job to be done, that the technology is there and that the economics are almost certainly there. If it has succeeded in doing that, you should need no bidding to assign the task of implementing these ideas within your own organisation. And the way to do this, as with everything, is through people. So start by finding yourself a computer-competent planner, and let him loose on your organisation. The cosmic dice will inevitably throw you a seven. He may not be able to do anything about your kitchen but he may be so profitable that you'll be able to buy a new house.

If you can find the right
person ...

Appendix 1

The Lord of the Files

Ye Fill up the Gaps in our Files

Matthew Arnold

This appendix is a postscript. It applies to computing generally and not just to projects. It is a bit of philosophy behind the use of computers generally after four decades of development; an attempt to explain what is happening today, and how to take best advantage of it.

An Ancient Tradition

The traditional means of providing data processing in an organisation has been to create well-structured systems with rules and regulations for use. Typically they are large, took years to develop, are (or should be) accompanied by lots of documentation, and are imposed upon the employees from above. There are well-understood reasons for this, and to most people it would be unthinkable to do it in any other way.

The fundamental reason for this monolithic imposition of computing is the software, not the hardware (at least today). By software we include both language and database structure. However, there are additional reasons, most of which come under the heading, company procedures; you use the immutability of the computer to run things your way.

Monolithic computing is efficient at the computer-technical level, but is it always efficient at the higher level of company business? If not, what can be done about it? How ought computing be provided? What ought to be the responsibility of the computing department?

The Employee Intrusion

To help answer these questions let us ask questions about what you expect of the employees in your company, and examine their relationship to the computer. Do you really want them to follow precise procedures, as though they were an extension of the computer itself? Or do you want them to think for themselves and take initiative where appropriate? To what extent do you want them to do either? The extremes are slaves and anarchists, and many companies do consist of hordes of slaves run by an anarchist. However, I think it would be easily agreed that successful companies are those in which employees display a mode of behaviour right across the slave-anarchist spectrum.

Most companies have a mixture of requirements of their people. Many things have to be done in a strict way. Selling airline tickets, for example. Handling customers' accounts in a bank. Drilling holes in metal. But if we restrict our people to a fully-determined mode of operation, who is going to create the innovation that a successful company needs to stay competitive? The managing director? The director of research? The company planner? Is innovation something you can legislate for? Do good ideas increase in number as you get older?

If you agree that innovation is something that you would like from everyone, then perhaps one way of encouraging it would be to relax the strait-jacket imposed by the computer. I'm not suggesting that you let everyone sell tickets in their own sweet way, but that in addition to the inevitable *procedural* systems you make available *personal* systems. You make it possible for each human element in the company to create his own "initiative" system; his own unique way of working with the corporate information, subject only to the limitations imposed by considerations of security.

Recipe versus Blueprint

At this point I would like to introduce a new discussion. In his excellent book, *The Blind Watchmaker* (Longman, 1986), Richard Dawkins considers the difference between a blueprint and a recipe. A blueprint tells you exactly how the final product shall look; size, shape, weight, functionality, with all due precision. On the other hand a recipe merely tells you how to make it. It prescribes materials, temperatures and times, but it says nothing about where the nuts and raisins must be located, and does not require precision as to height or diameter of the cake. No two cakes are identical, even though there may be a strong resemblance between the one being baked at Pompeii and one you may eat today.

A monolithic computer system is the result of a blueprint. Following the analogy, what sort of program would a recipe correspond to? And would it produce a better result?

The PC Intrusion

To try to answer these questions consider the intrusion of the personal computer. What is it about the PC that has allowed it to take off like wild-fire? Well, for one thing it is cheap. For another, it is fairly easy to handle. You don't have to know much about computers to be able to use it. But I would hazard the guess that the real attraction is that you are allowed to do pretty much what you like with it. You don't have to ask anyone's permission. It doesn't dictate to you. You decide yourself how to use it, and in doing so you evolve your own way of corporate life. You use computer power to help you do your job better in your own sweet way.

If you think then of lots of PCs in an organisation as extensions of the individual personalities of their owners, each being used in a different way, each an element of a local dynamic part of the company, you could think of this computer activity as a combination of ingredients and temperatures. You could think of this micro data activity as a sort of turbulent baking process, each individual responsible for his crumb or nut, with no overall blueprint specifying where the crumbs or nuts should be.

So, if we think of monolithic computing as resulting from a blueprint, we can think of personal computing as the result of a recipe (even though no one has actually written it down). And both have a place in the total scheme of things.

Who Delivers your Newspaper?

Another analogy is the supply of newspapers in a large city. Take London, for example. Every morning ten million people wake up to find the newspaper sitting on their doorstep. Yet no one organises it. There is no newspaper supremo sitting in some office in Whitehall responsible for the supply of newspapers to the population of London. If there were the result would be chaos. That's how they do things in Russia, and five decades after the war they are still queueing for everything they need.

The reason why newspapers get delivered reliably to the citizens of London is that the newspaper requirements-supply dynamics in each small locality are managed locally. In the same way as cells in fingers, ears and kneecaps are locally managed but build up into a body system, local newspaper management builds up into a body system.

Every morning ten million people wake up to find the
newspaper sitting on their doorstep

 Similarly, PCs in an organisation are locally managed, yet to a growing extent they build up into a corporate system.

But there is a problem with PCs. As isolated data-handlers they don't
make it easy to share data. By definition they don't have direct access
to corporate data. But it is often access to data captured by someone
else that a person needs. Fingers, ears and kneecaps do a lot of work
locally, however they all have access to the body's central mind/brain
database. Why not PCs?

The essential thing about the PC is that it is personal, and the owner
can very easily load it with local, personal functions. But this is no
reason for making it *isolated*. On the contrary, the more data a PC can
access the more value it will be to its owner.

And Who Delivers Your Data?

Now what should the role of the computing department be? Traditionally it has had the responsibility of providing system products. That is
to say, it has taken customer specifications and from them developed
systems that take in data and provide results in a more or less immut-

able way. Only very slowly have traditional systems evolved according to user requirements. And there are well-understood reasons for this, not least being the software, as we said at the beginning. Another factor has been the limitations of user understanding and acceptance. But we are undergoing dramatic change in both these factors. The advent of the PC has revolutionised end-user software, enabling user understanding to undergo a radical improvement. Indeed, quite frankly, in many installations we computer people have been overtaken by our customers. The new generation of users is impatiently chafing at the bit (joke), creating a demand for service that we have never experienced before. (In England there is currently a project under way for businessmen to attend computer school taught by schoolboys after hours!)

The central computing departments have traditionally supplied system products; combinations of data and operations on that data, leading to reports of one sort and another. Now there is no doubt that some of the data operations are technologically quite complicated, and have to be programmed by specialists. But many of them are really very simple, and are only a matter of combining data in a database in a variety of simple ways in order to produce a report. Given decent end-user tools, a non-computer person can easily learn these tools and create his own, tailor-made output.

As data expertise increases amongst the users the role of the computing department is inevitably to retreat closer and closer to the database and make the company information available in raw unprocessed form. The true role of today's computing department is to be the Lord of the Files; the trustee of the company's corporate information, supplying it to whoever needs it, to whoever is allowed to use it, to do with it whatever they think is best for the company, and to make its availability effortless on the part of the user. As time goes on, ancient data will be removed, or in some way amalgamated with the modern, minimising the natural growth of the database hardware.

The Lord of the Files would also give advice to company employees concerning PC and software tools, even to the extent of suggesting, in all modesty, an occasional company standard. He would also perform a function that the PC salesman never tells you about, either because he doesn't know about it himself, or he doesn't want to confuse you with the realities of life. The problem is that in the central computer room the men in the white coats do a lot for you that you are blissfully unaware of. They look after your data for you. They keep it safe from moths, dust, spies, viruses and acts of the electricity company. Whenever you return to it, it is exactly as you left it. But if you run your own isolated PC you have to do this for yourself. In all probability you'll discover the need for systematic archiving of your data with your first disaster, by which time it will be too late. A PC connected to the central machine enables your data to be archived automatically. It combines the best of both worlds - professional operations and personal use.

However -

Nothing comes without a price. Technology is neutral and can be used for good or ill. People can write programs that produce inaccurate results either by accident or deliberately, and the printed page has a dangerous authoritative effect on the mind. The plotted page is even worse; if it's in colour it must be right. Older, and therefore possibly senior, people often have difficulty learning new tricks. It is a duty of Computing to help them; you can't just open up the database and shout out come and get it. Some people, on the other hand, let the computer dominate them. They wind up producing nothing at all for their employer. The problem with computers is that they are fun.

So, with caution -

Let data initiative be the name of the game. While the central imposition of computing will probably be always with us the era of individual initiative is here to supplement and catalyse it. Technologically this means no more than simply attaching PCs to a central database, providing for local computing wherever possible, central number-crunching wherever necessary, and a vast (cheap), ever-growing base of information collected by the company to be used by its employees as they think fit. And the whole contraption shall be *seamless*; the individual will not have to be a computer expert to move back and forth between PC and central computer.

In short, the PC provides the individual with the freedom to compute. But don't provide that freedom at the price of the denial of data. Instead, make the PC a PT, a personal *terminal*, a work station attached to the company's database, choc-full of end-user software. Hire good people, give them the technology of data initiative, stand back and let them build a better company for you. I don't know how to solve many of the problems this will cause, but I do know that they are better problems to have on balance than the ones we used to have in the bad old monolithic days. You won't have a perfect company, but you will have a better one.